Million Dollar Websites

Million Dollar Websites

Build a Better Website Using Best Practices of the Web Elite in E-Business, Design, SEO, Usability, Social, Mobile and Conversion

REBECCA MURTAGH

Library of Congress Control Number: 2013931814

Murtagh, Rebecca
Million Dollar Websites : Build a Better Website Using Best Practices of the Web Elite in E-Business, Design, SEO, Usability, Social, Mobile and Conversion / Rebecca Murtagh

Published in the United States by Earl Press, New York
Includes bibliographic references.
ISBN 978-0-9889420-2-8
1. Website Planning.   2. Business Management.   3. Website Design.
4. Internet Marketing.   5. Search Engine Optimization.
6. Marketing Management.

"An investment in knowledge pays the best interest."

- Benjamin Franklin

*Dedicated to all who influence, challenge and inspire me
to do "good", and be "better" every day!*

Acknowledgements

Writing a book is an exciting proposition that becomes downright intimidating when it comes to publishing for the entire world to see. It is natural to reflect on the sources of encouragement and inspiration that led you to take on such an endeavor.

There are so many people who have influenced my journey to this point. Many saw qualities in me that would take much longer for me appreciate about myself.

For all their love and encouragement, I thank my mom, who has always believed in me; my husband, who is my greatest supporter and best friend; my brother, who has been steadfast in his support throughout life's many adventures; my son, who is the joy of my life; my cousin, who enthusiastically cheers me on in every endeavor I pursue; and, to my father, who didn't live long enough to enjoy the fruits of his labor and love.

This book began in the back of my mind many years ago. Fellow authors Guy Kawasaki, Seth Godin, Rob Garner, Shawn Welch, Erik Qualman and Shawn Rorick have led the way, giving me the courage to come out from behind the shadows to enthusiastically share my knowledge and perspective with others.

Thanks to Hugo (Buddy) Walpurgis, Adam Ellenbogen, Cliff Butler, and all the many talented technologists I have had the good fortune to work with over the years at WebWay, Harte Hanks, Wave Systems and through clients of my own firm, Karner Blue Marketing, LLC, who have taught me so much through collaboration in creating so many innovative and cutting-edge solutions over the years.

Gratitude to Kristine Schachinger, a smart professional who so generously supports her peers in the web industry. A sincere thank you to Mike DeBritz, who has nudged me every step of the way since we "white boarded" the outline of this book.

And, I thank you – the reader!
I sincerely hope you find this book useful in achieving your goals.

Table of Contents

Introduction:

About This Book

If you were born after 1990, you probably can't even imagine what life was like before the Internet. During its infancy, it was difficult to find value on the web, and most human interaction was confined to newsgroups. I remember receiving a T-shirt from Spiegel in the 1990s just for giving them my email address. I honestly don't recall whether I ever did receive an email from them after opting in. My, how times have changed!

That seems a lifetime ago. I'm sure I am not alone when I admit having difficulty remembering what it was like to run a business, to network, to deploy marketing, advertising, sales, or customer service, or to run day-to-day operations before the Internet. Can you imagine doing your job, finding information, or corresponding with colleagues, friends, and family without the web? Probably not, and exactly why I've written this book. Websites are not only here to stay, they are a permanent, vital, active extension of your business.

In the early days, many thought the Internet would be a passing fad. Even Microsoft co-founder and CEO Bill Gates is quoted as saying in 1993, *"The Internet? We are not interested in it."*

Sounds crazy now, right?

Mr. Gates was not alone. Businesses of all sizes were skeptical of the medium and extremely cautious about investing in what many saw as a passing fad, a flash in the pan. Few could envision the Internet as a platform that would serve as an extension of their business, let alone as the primary source of business.

In the 1990s most organizations assigned all things Internet to their IT teams. Surprisingly, even today some organizations continue to maintain the theory that if you accessed the Internet through computers, only technology professionals could leverage the platform. However, the website has become so much more.

Over the years, I have witnessed countless organizations struggle with their websites. To many, the website is an unwieldy expense and a source of headaches and stress, rather than the self-supporting business asset it should be.

Despite the evolution of the digital landscape, websites are often created the way brochures, magazines and sales sheets are traditionally published in a traditional publishing model. When approached as a permanent, published communication, rather than a dynamic, interaction with the brand, organizations are doomed, having to continually invest in repair and correction, rather than building upon the success of a website that met their needs from the beginning. Costly mistakes are commonly made, many of which could have been avoided if they had been better informed.

If they had access to the information you hold in your hand at this very moment, their fate might be quite different. I wish I could have saved them all that time and turmoil. If they had the information in this book, they might have made better decisions about deciding what to build, and who should build it and how, deliberately guiding the creation of a website that would support the bottom line.

Over the years I have created a methodology that integrates the best of what worked on a $1 million dollar budget website and many, many websites of all sizes throughout many industries since. What I have learned from my peers is that they deploy very similar methods to serve their employer or client. The only problem is the recipients of these methods are among the largest businesses and brands on the Internet. Very little of how these websites deliver the results they do has been shared, until now.

I Can Keep a Secret

I will be sharing insights that many in the web industry covet as industry secrets. In fact, some believe that access to such knowledge should be limited to the confines of well-compensated client relationships. I have shared so much of what is contained in this book in bits and pieces with clients and non-clients over the years, but never as part of one conversation.

More than one client has called me their "secret weapon" when it comes to SEO and digital strategy. These organizations come from a wide variety of highly competitive industries, including multi-national consumer brands, technology companies, retail store chains, e-commerce stores, small businesses, and service businesses. Because they do not want competitors to know who they are working with, they often request exclusivity and complete confidentiality. So, although I do not identify specific clients, I do my best to share insights in a way that benefits many.

Based on Experience

Fortunate enough to have worked with so many clients, agencies, designers, developers, new media firms, and the "web elite" over the years, I have seen common challenges come up over and again. How these challenges are resolved often impact the performance and ROI of the website. Through trial, error, and testing, I perfected a methodology over the years to serve my clients. Now virtually any organization can apply to "up their game" online with what I and the web elite have proven to be effective.

Silent No More

Nothing is more frustrating and disappointing than to learn that an organization has invested valuable time and capital, only to discover that they settled for less than they thought they would get, got less than they paid for, or ended up with a website that did not deliver what they needed to be competitive or successful. Far too many companies have their eye on the prize, without preparing for the fight. These scenarios have kept me quite busy over the years. However, there are only so many organizations I can help. The vulnerabilities I identify within the website process in this book are systemic and, quite frankly, benefit a large number of web professionals. The less their clients know, the more profitable their business is. The web elite frequently reveal sub-standard practices in their blogs, presentations, and interactions with clients. Unfortunately, "status quo" continues. Some of the most harmful assumptions continue to drive the website process of those less informed. When it all falls apart later, the reputation of those applying best practices are dragged down with those who simply allude to these methods and just can't resist doing whatever they want, regardless of the cost to the brand or business.

What Do You Really Want?

Your website will reflect exactly what you ask for. The problem is many organizations do not know how to articulate what they need, so the website is delivered as the vision was communicated.

After working with numerous organizations, from large corporation to solo-entrepreneurs and everything in between in the United States and Canada, I have learned a thing or two about what makes a great website. I also have had the distinct pleasure of working with some of the most talented professionals in the industry.

Whether you are building your website yourself, delegating it to in-house resources, hiring an outside vendor, or some combination thereof, I will show you how to articulate exactly what you need from your website and how to make sure you get it.

The Website Decision

This book begins with the premise that you understand the importance of a website. If you remain unconvinced that a website is vital to your business or brand, I encourage you to read on. You will likely grow to understand the value of a website. However, my focus is on how to leverage the website as a business asset, rather than making the case for creating a website.

Caution

I will show you how to avoid some of the most common and costly mistakes made by organizations when it comes to creating or re-designing a website. You may have experienced some of these already, some you will likely encounter in the future, and some you may not have even recognized as mistakes until after reading this book.

The Missing Link

Ever feel that something is "missing" with your website? You may not be sure how to articulate exactly what it is, but when your investment exceeds the return generated by the website, you instinctively know something went wrong. The information I provide in this book is designed to help you become more engaged with the website so that you can more easily identify what may be wrong, and how to fix it.

Sometimes, even after you figure out exactly where your website is lacking, you will find yourself "stuck" with what you have because of contractual or financial limitations. There is nothing more discouraging than to feel unable to make the improvements required to compete online. My goal is to provide you with insight and best practices that you can scale to make more informed decisions when creating a digital destination that is able to adapt and meet the growing demands of your customers.

Whether your role is in the C-Suite or you are creative, technical, design, or marketing professional, my goal is to assist you in mastering the website, the digital extension of your business. The website is an asset, as vital to your success as the business plan, people, building, and processes you depend upon every day to build a sustainable business.

It's a Matter of Perspective

Organizations typically lean on one perspective when it comes to the website. Some still believe that the website is a function of technology and approach the website as a platform for deployment of intense programming, software, and hardware. Many organizations approach website creation in silos.

In fact, I was recently approached by an organization whose board of directors wanted to have an e-business strategist come in and help them migrate ownership of the website from a function of the information technology team to the marketing department.

Others view the website as a creative expression, making a beautiful website the primary goal. Then there are the marketing departments who know what they expect from the website, but because of the volume of moving parts on their plate, often make big decisions on the fly, without a full appreciation of the impact of their choices. And then there are those who will put all their eggs in the SEO basket to achieve top rank, only to be left wondering why they cannot convert visitors to customers and fully realize the return on that investment.

Focusing on any one of these approaches often creates a void that fails to connect the dots between form, function, and performance. I will show you how to create a website that is inherently capable of supporting business objectives through strategic integration of best practices, emerging technology, design, usability, and optimization.

Whether you have historically deferred to in-house technology, marketing, or creative teams; outsourced to an agency, web design and development firm; built the website yourself; or some combination thereof, you can achieve a winning website by applying methods proven to deliver results. You must first be willing to adopt a new way of thinking.

Sympatico

A holistic perspective of your digital presence is imperative. The best, most effective websites feature more than good design, cool technology, or top-ranking position in search. The best websites evolve from the integration of business strategy, technology, design, function, visibility, conversion, and deliberate orchestration with off-line activities related to operations, customer service, marketing, advertising, and promotion in order to achieve pre-determined goals.

Because I have worked with a $1 million dollar budget but also worked on websites of modest means, I have firsthand knowledge of how best practices can be effectively applied and scaled, regardless of how big (or small) your organization or budget is.

I want you to expect more. I want you to get more. Your website can and will support your goals when you are able to define your needs and identify the best solution. Your website is as important as choosing your business name, office or store location, logo, and the individuals you hire to make your business profitable. Just as you procure equipment, staff, and services, due diligence will pay off when building a high-performing website.

The Life of the Website Begins When the Project Ends

For years clients have asked me to help them fix failing websites created by vendors with great reputations and impressive client rosters. The problem is, many designers, programmers, agencies, and new media firms have created profitable businesses by delivering "just enough." Performance is not on their radar because the day the website goes "live" is the day their work is done and they move on to the next. For the brand reliant upon the website as a business asset, the day that the website goes live is just the beginning. The two do not align. We will address the fatal flaw in how websites are created today, and how to avoid the costly mistakes that so many before you have had to learn the hard way.

Raising the Bar

I encourage organizations to take ownership of the website from the top down, and I make my living driving organizational goals from the C-Suite through every decision related to the website.

When you approach the website as a business asset, you do not have to learn a new language or create an expert to articulate what your business needs to succeed online. What you do need is to lead the dialogue from a strategic business perspective. Then, and only then, will you be able to expect the website to fulfill its potential in supporting your goals.

Any Size, Any Budget

Million Dollar Websites shows you how to scale methods used to create high-performance, big-budget websites to a website of any size or budget.

Just as there are fundamentals of architecture that apply, regardless of the size of the structure, there are fundamentals of websites that apply to any size of website. My primary objective is to empower you to lead the creation of a successful website, regardless of industry, size, or budget.

Ready? Let's get started!

Chapter 1 :

The Million Dollar Website

Congratulations! Your decision to read this book is the first step toward creating a better website capable of supporting your goals. This is no small feat as anyone who has had a hand in building a website will tell you. Connecting the dots between a great business concept and a great website is easier said than done.

What does "Million Dollar Website" mean to you? Whether you hope to make a million dollars, invest a million dollars, or are simply seeking insight that will help you achieve your goals, I have written this book for you.

There's no need to reinvent the wheel. You can build a better website by leveraging best practices shared by those who have mastered the website, the web elite. You can avoid common mistakes made each and every day by other brands, as well as by experienced web professionals, top-notch agencies, web designers, and new media firms and teams tasked with building websites.

You may wonder why I am so sure these seemingly knowledgeable professionals are making mistakes. I have the pleasure, and challenge, of working with web professionals of every imaginable skill level, every day.

The Odds

Chances are you have, or will have, invested a great deal into your website. Unfortunately, chances are even greater that the website you end up with may not be capable of delivering the results you set out to achieve.

Dirty Little Secret

I'll let you in on the web industry's dirty little secret. A shockingly high percentage of websites never deliver results. Because of the enormous demand for websites and the availability of fundamental tools to create a website, just about anyone can deliver something that resembles a website. The unsuspecting website customer often settles for much less than they need, and pays for far more than they receive.

The way brands have been conditioned to approach the website has become a fundamental barrier to realizing the full potential of the website and return on investment.

This book empowers brands and businesses of all sizes to become better consumers of website service, whether in-house, outsourced, or a combination thereof.

It Is Time to Update the Definition of a Website

Currently, the Achilles heel of the web industry is that the definition of a quality website is subject to perception. Wikipedia defines the website as "*a set of related web pages containing content such as text, images, video, audio, etc.*"

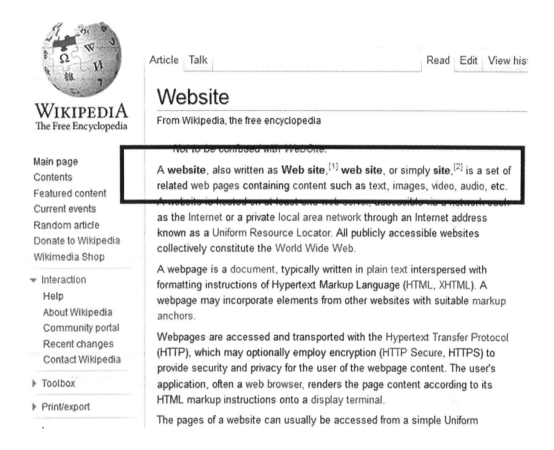

This definition is not only outdated, it greatly reduces the perceived value of what has become one of the most powerful assets a business can leverage in today's marketplace.

Anyone who uses the web knows that a website is much more than a collection of pages and assets. The website is an environment that enables interaction, generates data, and facilitates the creation of relationships between the brand and its customers.

A more accurate definition of today's website would be:

"A digital environment capable of delivering information and solutions and promoting interaction between people, places, and things to support the goals of the organization it was created for."

Kind of changes your perception of the inherent power of a website, doesn't it?

This entire book is dedicated to elevating your view and expectations that the website can support your goals.

What a Website Should Be

An effective website should reach target audiences, engage visitors, and effectively convert those visitors to customers. It marries style, function, and performance. It rarely costs more than its less-stellar counterparts and successfully delivers a return on investment.

Unfortunately, such websites are rare, and mediocre websites are far too common. It does not have to be this way. Building a better website is not rocket science, voodoo, or black magic. Successful websites are products of strategic planning, the balance of priorities, and a firm definition of requirements that drive design, SEO, mobile, content, and social media decisions. This book provides a framework you can use to create such a website.

Pretend for a moment that the sky is the limit for your website budget. What would you want your website to deliver? Would you want to generate revenue, launch a brand, wow the audience, create community, or build a loyal audience? Maybe you would like to reduce operational costs, improve customer loyalty, educate staff, or streamline process. Would you want to cultivate leads, sell, up-sell, cross-sell, or cultivate marketing data and consumer intelligence that can be sold? What about integrating legacy software, hardware, or inventory? Maybe you would like to launch new products or services, differentiate yourself from your competitors, promote sales, reduce the cost of customer acquisition, streamline operations, or some combination of the above?

Missing Ingredient

Surprisingly, those seeking to build a new website rarely articulate key performance indicators (KPIs) to those they will assign the task of creating the environment that will achieve those goals. Even those who have presented a "wish list" to the web team or vendors will be faced with multiple decisions that can, and often do, derail the primary function of the website.

I have not written this book to discredit the industry or scare you away from the process. My goal is to enable you to own the process that will create the website you require to achieve key objectives.

The Quality Website

In April 2012 Google updated its search engine algorithm with an update called Penguin. At the same time, the head of Google's Web Spam Team, Matt Cutts, shared a post outlining how these updates are designed to reward "Quality Websites." Search engines Google, Yahoo, and Bing value quality websites and have each published guidelines that reflect best practices that have been known to the web elite for many years. We explore the search implications of the quality website in the SEO chapter. However, because these "quality guidelines" resonate with best practices developed and proven to be effective over the years, they warrant serious consideration.

Quality = Cost?

Never is it suggested you must invest great sums of money to create a quality website. Website visitors, and search engines for that matter, could care less about what you invested to build the website. It is the website itself that will determine success.

The web elite know that success online has little to do with what you spend. How you invest what you will spend makes all the difference.

A successful website leverages opportunities inherent to the digital landscape to connect and build relationships, one visitor at a time. The quality website adheres to industry best practices to improve compliance and performance.

In today's competitive digital economy, performance is more important than ever. Unfortunately, measureable results elude many brands because they did not know how to ensure the process produced the website that would deliver exactly that.

Not So Common

Ever hear the phrase "common sense is not all that common"? The same could be said about best practices in web creation.

I have had the honor of working and collaborating with some of the most talented and knowledgeable professionals in the web industry since the 1990s. Those whom I call the "web elite" are highly experienced practitioners that deliver results on the web each and every day. The insights and expertise these professionals share has created a professional threshold of methodology and performance that has eluded much of the web industry. As a result, expectations are lowered and quality diminishes, even in the hands of award-winning agencies, designers, and developers.

Having been fortunate enough to have worked on a $1 million dollar budget website as well as the "no budget" website (and just about everything in between), I can say with complete confidence that money does not necessarily translate to performance. The best practices I share with you in this book are applied every day by the web elite, and they can be applied to build a website that supports your business objectives, regardless of how large, or small, your website budget may be.

Chapter 2:

Money Pit vs. Money Tree

Does the website pay for itself? Does it contribute to the bottom line in a positive way? Does it differentiate brand, products, and services from your competitors? Is it easy to navigate and does it offer value and convert visitors to customers? Or, will the website demand a seemingly endless stream of time, money, and resources, and still fail to deliver results?

There are several key factors that will determine whether the website will be a money pit, or a money tree.

Ownership = Success

Now that we have established that the website is much more than pages, links, images, and posts, it is imperative that we focus on what the website can—and should—be. The first step is to shift ownership of the process from those building the website to the organization the website is built for.

To those seeking guidance and assistance from web professionals, the web industry has resembled the wild, Wild West creating an unwieldy landscape of service providers competing for business to create the website without standards or means to measure quality or performance. Those hiring web professionals or vendors are required to do so based on faith and trust, unless they are prepared to drive the process.

Chances for success amplify significantly when ownership of the website process shifts from the web team or vendor to those vested in the success of the business. Seemingly simple, this shift requires a new approach to the website process.

Fully Invested

Far too often, once the site goes live, organizations begin to anxiously await results that may never come—not because the vendor couldn't create what they needed, but rather because those who would rely upon the performance of the website were unable to articulate what would be required in order to realize success. It is imperative that the website reflect each part of the organization that will rely upon the performance of the website. If your customers currently rely upon customer support offline, you can bet they will expect that support to be accessible through the website. If the business depends on booking appointments, presenting this function online greatly enhances the website's value to customers.

Offering value to those who will visit the website greatly increases the value of the website to the brand. We discuss how to solicit and leverage insights from the experts within your organization in the chapter on Strategy.

Means to No End

Many organizations believe that all they need is to create the website. They make the fatal mistake of investing their entire web budget into the design or development of the website, neglecting to plan for ongoing optimization, updates, content creation, social integration, and analysis. By the time the website is complete, they have already spent any budget, schedule, and energy they have allocated for the website. So, instead of viewing the website as the beginning of the digital investment, many choose to "let it ride" over investing in a maintenance program, regular analysis, and ongoing updates.

This fatal mistake has led to the demise of even well-executed websites.

Only when resources are properly allocated to ongoing assessment, planning, optimization, and management of the website can the website fulfill its potential.

The web elite know that the creation of the website is just the beginning. Because the website will compete in the ever-changing digital landscape (with or without recognition of the brand), it must become a dynamic reflection of the business and the marketplace it operates in. The organization that embraces this approach and supports the entire life cycle of a website will enjoy better results across all functions.

Not As Easy As It Looks

If one were to listen to the hype, it might seem as if anyone can create a website. Free websites are available as a by-product of hosting accounts or advertising packages. At the next level, cheap templates and themes for open-source platforms like WordPress, Drupal, and Joomla have made it easy for just about anyone to create a website. Those who graduate to the next level of licensing a platform or building it from scratch often do so believing the website can be executed well by anyone.

This false sense of confidence has led many brands to demand key in-house personnel, and sometimes the president of the company, to become so distracted with learning the website process that the business suffers. This can be a fatal mistake.

A massive proliferation of web providers has stemmed from this same false sense of confidence. True, many can design or build a website. However, very few look beyond the website as a means for them to make a living. As a result, the industry is filled with professionals and vendors with ample construction skills, but who lack the experience and expertise to architect, decorate, and maintain the property for the good of the brand.

Bridging the gap between the website and the success of the brand can be daunting, even for web professionals. We must explore the key decisions within the website process that create opportunities to elevate value and improve performance of a website.

You Get What You Pay For

Far too many legitimate businesses are being wooed into thinking that a website created by their domain registrar, advertising platform, or hosting company will enable them to compete online. The harsh truth is you get what you pay for, unless you are prepared to leverage these tools in the scope of an overall strategy. Without fully understanding how the web works and how to leverage the platform or design of choice, you are destined to be disappointed and frustrated. If it sounds too good to be true, it probably is.

Choosing the right platform on which to build your website is an important decision, which we discuss later in the book. For now, you simply need to recognize that until you have identified exactly what you expect from the website and how to plan to achieve those objectives, selecting a website platform or vendor is a waste of your valuable time and money.

Bottom Line Is the Bottom Line

Whether you start from scratch and code in HTML; choose an open-source platform like WordPress or Drupal; or hire a web designer, local firm, or world-class agency, the website will only be as good as you are prepared to make it.

The reality is that even no-cost or low-cost approaches can be effective in the hands of a prepared individual. By the time you have read this book, you will know enough to build a better website. Whether it is your first or tenth website, my goal is to prepare you to make good decisions. You will look good, the brand will look good, and everyone wins.

The World Is Your Oyster

Once you decide to approach the website as a business asset and own the process, the world of vendors opens up to you. There are countless ways to get online, but very few, if any, will connect the dots between the business and the digital platform.

The quality of services being provided by web professionals varies greatly. There are literally millions of professionals and companies that sell website services. Some are qualified, some are not. Most organizations are qualified to deliver a quality website to some degree. However, it is not the skill of web professionals that is the greatest barrier to creating a winning website. The biggest reason most websites fail to fulfill their potential is that it was not treated like the business asset it is before it was placed in the hands of the builders (web designers, developers, SEOs, scripters, copywriters, etc.).

Most website professionals are not in the "bottom-line" business, they are in the website-building business. Building a website is like building a house. Far too many websites fail because decorating began before the blueprint was drawn.

You have to know what you want before an architect can bring your vision to life. You would never hire the builder of a home without deciding on a location, drawing up blueprints, and specifying the mechanicals that will run the household. Only after those decisions are made, can the builder, plumber, electrician, and interior designer do what they do best. The website requires the same consideration. You must enter into the construction phase of the website prepared and in control with a vision, a plan, and a blueprint. Once you take ownership of the process and are prepared to drive the process and manage the asset over time, the possibilities are endless.

Not Mind Readers

When the client (internal or external) has not done due diligence, they often turn to the web team to figure it out. Web professionals have articulated to me time and time again that their greatest challenge is trying to read their clients' minds. When you enter into the construction phase of the website and do not know what you want or need, the web professionals make decisions for you. This puts the power on the wrong side of the relationship.

Most web professionals do not want to be responsible for this aspect of the website. They admit they are not qualified or interested in leading the discussion from a business perspective. This is exactly why business strategy and KPIs are omitted from the process most of the web industry works from.

In the absence of direction, most web professionals default to the discussion that asks how many pages the website will be, what the budget is, what platform will be used, or what kind of visual presentation is envisioned. By now you can already appreciate that these discussions are valid once you are prepared to proactively guide the discussion, and not a moment before.

Great Expectations

Website designers, architects, programmers, scripters, SEOs, and copywriters expect you to know what you want BEFORE you come to them. They would tell you this themselves if they thought they could without losing your business. Instead, they improvise and embrace the project. You cannot afford for this to happen.

The website is more likely to deliver your intended results when clear direction guides key decisions. Those working for an agency, web design firm, SEO company, web development firm, or independent vendor state they could do their job much more effectively if the client knew what they wanted. You will be able to articulate what you require from the website after you read this book.

Time Is Money

Many organizations invest in website designs, redesigns, and optimization again and again, only to discover that the website costs more than it delivers. Investing in multiple iterations over time becomes extremely expensive, not just from a monetary perspective, but also from a competitive standpoint. In today's quickly evolving business landscape, there is little time to experiment your way to success.

Good or Great Websites Are Rare

Far too many websites fail. Unfortunately most organizations are not able to determine whether their website is successful or not. Only after losing its search position or market share, becoming undeliverable on mobile devices, or failing to convert visitors to customers does the website warrant scrutiny. After all, if it looks great and has all the required information, all is well, right? This is a dangerous place to be. Your success is uncertain unless you know that the website is doing what it was created to do. Otherwise, why bother?

A great website doesn't just happen. The web elite will tell you that a winning website is the product of a succession of good decisions. I will prepare you for these decisions.

Knowledge Is Power

Ever hear the saying, the more you know the more you realize you don't know? I humbly admit to this each and every day. Even after 17 years in the digital space and with more than 25 years in business management, communication design, marketing, and sales, I find that the more I learn, the more I want (and need) to learn.

Many very expensive, well-designed, or feature-rich websites fail, or fall short of delivering the results they were designed to deliver because decisions were made without proper preparation. I cannot tell you how many times new clients have sought my help to save their business and salvage their website. Some were large brands you would probably recognize. Many were aspiring entrepreneurs who invested every dime they had into purchasing a website when they didn't understand what they were buying. They based their trust on assumptions based on their frame of reference, which simply was not enough.

The digital landscape changes very quickly, which means the landscape in which your website must compete is also changing every day. There is a tremendous volume of data and information being disseminated every second of every day. Trying to absorb it all when a new website is to be created is like trying to take a sip from a fire hydrant. Because you likely wear other hats and have other responsibilities, it is impossible to know everything you need to know about the digital landscape to make decisions that will enable you to compete online, regardless of how big your budget—or that of your competitor—is. And, truth be told, reading will not be enough. However, the knowledge you possess about your business and your understanding of the website as a business asset can be enough to achieve the desired results.

Knowledge is the great equalizer. The more you know, the more you can expect, even when the team or assets you choose—or are required to work with—are less than perfect.

Confidence

This is a delicate subject, but it needs to be addressed. The more you know, the more confident you will become. In fact, the reason I wrote this book was to enable you to become more knowledgeable so that you may make website-related decisions with more confidence. However, there is a balance between knowledge and expertise.

If all it took was a little bit of knowledge to be successful, everyone would make millions on the Internet. This is exactly why so many think they can build a good website even though most have no business doing it for themselves, let alone selling their wares to others.

Even with all the information I have provided in this book, there are sure to be unique situations you will face that will require additional information. And, sure enough, tomorrow some new protocol or competitive challenge will force you to dive in deeper than the depth of your knowledge will enable you to go. This is when you must be willing to seek the insight and guidance of trusted experts that have historical reference and that have built, tested, and proven methods that can be used to address the specific needs of your business or brand.

Expertise Comes from Experience

I recall an experience I had in a website-planning meeting with a multi-national client and their agency that would be building the website. I was responsible for SEO. We all flew in from our respective cities to meet at the agency's headquarters. The agency had flown in a young man from the West Coast as their new SEO expert. He challenged everything I recommended relating to website architecture, content, and specifically my recommendation against building the agency's pitch for a FLASH website, beginning each contradiction with the phrase, "I've read…" I respectfully listened and responded that although reading may provide insight, only implementation, testing, and analysis can be relied upon when forming an opinion when it comes to SEO or any other method used in the digital space. Despite my recommendation and the inexperience of this individual, the client went ahead and built the FLASH site, which became an even greater liability when Google preview could not display the website, and those on Apple mobile devices could not see the website at all. Fortunately, the client's confidence in my knowledge grew and the client did finally replace the FLASH website, three years later.

My point in sharing this is to illustrate that unless you live and breathe the industry, there is no way you can know everything you need to know. And, chances are good that you may not even know enough to recognize solid recommendations when they are presented to you. Trust will play a large role in the decisions you make.

Trust in your knowledge of your business and in those with the expertise you will rely upon to make informed decisions.

No Code Required

You do not need to learn a new language to communicate effectively with those who will build the website. Whether you are the CEO, CMO, CFO, VP, director of marketing, sales, entrepreneur, or small business owner, I will show you how to apply best practices within a framework you can apply, over and again, to articulate what you need and expect from a website. I will share insights along the way based on many years of experience to enable you to connect the dots between best practices and practical application to your website.

The Internet Today: The Good, Bad, and the Ugly

The Good: The Internet has matured a great deal in recent years, making it easier than ever for brands to reach customers. In March 2012 there were 644 million websites on the web, according to Netcraft. Perhaps one of the most wonderful benefits of the saturation of the Internet is that many organizations seek to execute the same tasks online. The online community is continually creating a wealth of platforms, applications, services, and solutions that can help you deliver the functionality you seek much less expensively than in the past. Open-source platforms, the Cloud, plugins, widgets SAAS, and apps can elevate the functionality of your website at a fraction of the cost of building solutions yourself or hiring developers to build them for you. Of course there are times when custom development will be required. However, many core functions are easily accessible, with new developments every day (literally). Once you understand how to apply emerging and current technology to the best practices provided in this book, your website may fulfill its potential effectively and cost-efficiently.

The Bad: If your only goal for building a website is simply to get one out there, you very well may be wasting time and money. The Internet is a global network. Unless you proactively leverage every aspect of the website, it is destined to fade into oblivion.

Let me help you put this in perspective. While working with a CPA firm in the Midwest, I pointed out to them that without positioning the website with focus on the geographic marketplace they wished to limit their practice to, they were essentially competing against every CPA firm in the world. Geolocation is just one of the many factors required to put a website in the path of its customers.

A strategic plan will do more than geographically position the business. The website strategy will promote brand, differentiate the business from its competitors, reach target audiences, deliver value, and convert visitors to customers. I walk you through the strategic planning process in the chapter on Website Strategy.

The Ugly: Building websites has largely been reduced to a commodity business which has resulted in diminished value to the brand. The most common mistakes are made when the website has become a project and ownership is released to those without skin in the game. Some are distracted by bright shiny objects that diminish ROI and that result in a website that cannot fulfill its potential, requiring more time, money, and resources after the website goes live. This book will reveal how to overcome challenges most do not anticipate before they have a chance to derail the website mission.

Build It and They Will Come

Creating a winning experience for your customers will improve the potential for bottom-line results. Have you ever felt like Ray Kinsella (Kevin Costner) in *Field of Dreams*, courageously building your website, dreaming and hoping your customers will find it?

Wake Up!

Forget about the dream. I love an underdog as much as the next person, but the bitter truth is the days of "build it and they will come" are long gone. Accepting this approach with your company's website could be costly, or fatal.

Don't Settle

My goal is to help you avoid common thresholds of "settling" that may be presented to you. When you command power as the "master" of the website, you will be much more satisfied with website performance over time, I assure you.

Every chapter of this book is designed to empower you to confidently navigate the many decisions you will face when planning for and building a website. I realize that you may be familiar with some of what you read. Regardless, I want to encourage you to read through each chapter as there are valuable insights and examples that may alter or enhance your point of view.

Excellence on the Web

I have evaluated thousands of websites over the years, viewing source code, reading case studies, and testing methodologies. Completing my ninth year as an expert judge in 2012 for the Web Marketing Association's WebAwards, I, and other web expert judges, reviewed and scored websites from around the world in 96 categories on various criteria, including use of technology, content, innovation, usability, interaction with the website owner, etc. I have also done live site reviews at conferences, in seminars, with potential clients, as well as countless hours on my own analyzing, dissecting, and evaluating websites.

Just when I think I have seen it all, I am surprised at both ends of the spectrum—websites that raise the bar in demonstrating what a website is capable of and those that should never have seen the light of day.

Excellence Is Earned

Not every great website started out great. Most websites start out good and evolve to great over time.

Amazon.com is a fantastic example. A success story in its own right, the Amazon team obviously embraces the credo of continual improvement. As a result, one simple tweak to the Amazon.com user experience generated a $300 million dollar increase in revenue. We will look at this example more closely in the chapter on Usability and

Accessibility. I point this out to you now because it is important to view the website as a living environment that must be groomed and nurtured to fulfill its true potential. With the right direction, just about any website can be made great.

Everyone Makes Mistakes

"Perfect" does not exist in the digital world. Big brands and even the web elite make mistakes. So, rather than expecting to be flawless in the execution of your website, I would rather see you be bold and deliberate in your evaluation, analysis, and action to continually improve the user experience and performance.

The Million Dollar Dream

Every organization that builds a website has some level of expectation regarding the success of the website. For the lucky few who get it right, it is a dream. For the rest, the website becomes a recurring nightmare that literally keeps them up at night.

Many share the dream of building an Internet business based on a great idea. Many have great ideas. And, the media shares success stories that inspire others to stake their claim on the Internet. Unfortunately, few will succeed in effectively translating their ideas into a profitable venture. This is often due to the misconception that all it takes is a website when, in fact, even what appear to be the simplest of successful websites are a culmination of good planning, execution, and management.

"Results Not Typical"

This is one of those disclaimers you see for diet products, self-improvement programs, or "get-rich quick" schemes. It warns you that the success of a few is not what most should expect.

The same is true for a winning website. Millions of websites are built and updated every year. Yet, few can be considered successful—not because the business wasn't good, but because mistakes were made along the way that diminished the ability for the website to support the vision.

The web elite know that it takes a great deal of hard work to be successful online. Just as the reality show "The Biggest Loser" demonstrates, the winners are those who are willing to do what is demanded of them. There are no short cuts. And, even when you achieve a certain level of success, you must never stop striving to improve. You may not get rich right away, and the changes you make to tweak your website for better performance may not yield a $300 million dollar increase in sales like it did for Amazon, but you can most definitely be successful when you approach the website as a strategic business asset.

Assume Nothing

For those who have ever found themselves in the position of paying for a website only to find out later that they did not receive what they expected, or that the "experts" they trusted to deliver a winning website weren't so knowledgeable after all, this book is for you. It is my goal to provide you with insight that typically only the web elite are privileged to have, so that you can avoid making preventable mistakes.

Far too often, a distressed C-level executive or entrepreneur seeks my help to make sense of why they invested tens of thousands of dollars into a website that Google does not even see. Or, they were told they were purchasing a custom solution, only to find out they were sold a mere duplication of a template populated by the same content that hundreds or thousands of others have also been sold (not so custom).

Surprise!

After many years I am astounded by how many brands continue to be told after completion of the website project, that SEO was not provided. There is always some reasoning behind this 11th-hour surprise. Regardless of the excuse provided, the result is most often a sense of betrayal. The brand is then asked to dig into the budget to pay for SEO, just when they thought the project was finished. Every time I have heard this story, the client has told me that SEO was "discussed" during the planning phase, and they assumed it would be included. And, every one of these clients paid for a website void of search engine optimization.

The problem was not in the solution they were sold. The problem was they were not equipped with the knowledge to make an informed decision before signing off on the requirements for the website. This breaks my heart. There is no reason for any entrepreneur or business to find themselves in this position, ever. Watching businesses suffer from uninformed website decisions is among the most compelling reasons behind my decision to write this book.

Take Your Medicine

I cannot stress the following point enough. When you have qualified and invested in the advice and services of an expert, fill the prescription and follow the directions! I cannot tell you how often the web elite report that their clients will not implement the recommendations they provide. Or, the client implements only 20–30 percent of what is recommended and still expects 100 percent of the results. This happens far too often.

Just as you must fill and take the prescription your doctor gives you to eliminate an illness, just as you must exercise to improve cardiovascular health and flexibility, you must implement the prescription for your website and business—all of it. There are no short-cuts. There is no quick fix. You cannot expect 100 percent of the results if you are only willing to fill part of the prescription.

Information Is Key

There are a wide variety of solutions available to meet the needs of an organization of any size. The choices involved in planning a website often overwhelm those seeking the best solution for their needs. By the time you finish this book, you will be able to hone in on the solutions that will best serve your needs. I will show you that by approaching the website from a business perspective, you can apply methods that industry leaders (and likely your competitors) use to compete and win online.

More important than design, technical aptitude, or marketing prowess is information. Whether you are building your website or hiring others to build it for you, the more you know, the more you can expect to get what you want and need from your investment.

Now that you understand the challenges you face, let's talk about solutions!

Chapter 3:

Avoid Common and Costly Mistakes

Taking ownership of any website can be an intimidating endeavor, especially when you fully appreciate what is at stake. It requires time and energy to ensure it is capable of meeting your expectations.

Most businesses recognize the need to have a website, but few will fully leverage the website as a vital aspect of their brand, marketing, sales, customer service, operations, human resources, and financial performance. Many will place a heavy demand on the website, yet overlook some of the most strategic aspects required to achieve those expectations. They proceed with the website "project" before they are ready or able to clearly articulate what they expect, or need, the website to do.

According to Albert Einstein, the definition of *insanity* is doing the same thing over and over again, expecting different results. Consequently, approaching the website with the same failing process over and again is not only expensive, it is insane. Choices are made that are costly, or fatal, to the organization the website was built for, often beyond the awareness of the involved parties.

Every website has the potential to offer something unique from the millions of websites online. However, because the web industry has not kept up with how important the website is to the brand nor the growing expectations of Internet users, many websites will fail to meet their potential.

The web industry has produced a platform that favors execution over strategy, form, and function. Every day, unsuspecting organizations enter into the same cookie-cutter website process. As a result, unintended mistakes are made that often result in rebuilding a website sooner rather than later, again increasing the cost to the organization.

This book reveals pitfalls inherent to the typical website process, provides valuable insight, and promotes better decision-making. The more you know, the more effectively you can invest your time and money.

Over the years numerous organizations have approached me to improve the performance of their websites. As a result, several decisions and choices have become key indicators of success. How you approach your website will determine whether the website can, and will meet its potential.

Common mistakes are made by those new to the website process, experienced professionals, and a very large percentage of professional webmasters, designers, and developers. Large corporations and medium enterprises make many of the same mistakes you might expect from a small business or a start-up.

Large or small, your website goals will be well served if you avoid the following common mistakes:

1. Handing the Website Over

I am not suggesting you will not require website design, programming, SEO, copy writing, or marketing professionals. On the contrary, I believe because most organizations do not go through the website creation process often enough, the expertise of experienced professionals is invaluable. However, I do advocate that the website should never be handed off or assigned to an in-house team, vendor, or hybrid team without proper preparation and guidance from executive leadership.

Having been fortunate to have worked with organizations of all sizes—from Fortune 500 to start-ups and everything in between—I have led or been part of the website process in its various forms as the client, vendor, and consultant. Regardless of how the website was built, the "client," internal or external, is always the business that is reliant upon the website's performance to achieve mission-critical goals. The client has the most to gain, and the most to lose. It is imperative that the client own the process as the architect and view the web team as the builders. I explain this further in the chapter on Strategy.

Every organization's process is slightly different. However, when business objectives and user needs are used to develop website requirements before entering into website creation, matching talent and style is simplified and more cost-efficient.

When organizations defer to designers and developers, assumptions are made that will drive decisions that can and will impact the client's bottom. This is where most organizations lose control of the website as a business asset. Below are illustrations of how this has played out for businesses competing in the real -world.

Real-World Insight:
Brick and Mortar to Internet Retailer

I was approached by a retail company that had a similar problem. They had hired a programmer to customize a Yahoo Store to enable them to sell the same goods online that they sold in their brick-and-mortar stores. They were unable to compete in search and, like many brick-and-mortar retailers, wanted to grow their e-commerce revenues.

Upon evaluation, it was evident that the website literally copied data from other sources, which made it accurate, but rendered the site invisible in search. In addition, they had no competitive advantage to entice visitors to trust a brand they may never have heart of, and, they made no reference to their brick-and-mortar stores. So, they were unable to compete in local or national search. This is not uncommon. In fact, the reality is, these are not factors programmers are "wired" to think about. Their job lies in code and function, not competition, visibility, content, and conversion.

Real-World Insight: *Saving the Site for Singles*

A C-level executive of a large Internet matchmaking dating site approached my firm for assistance in SEO. They had identified search as a method to increase membership. Having hired several firms before, and having invested a great deal of money, they continued to struggle to achieve top search engine visibility as a single's destination site. Having been burned by what I call SEO "posers," they were understandably skeptical but decided to move forward. Upon initial review it became extremely clear that the only thing previous vendors had done was metadata, and much of it was done á la "black hat." I address the danger of this approach to search engine optimization in the chapter on SEO. However, search was not their greatest challenge. The website had not fully connected the dots among visitors, members, and revenue models in the user experience.

What began as a discussion based on their initial understanding of SEO expanded into discussion on e-business strategy and how the website could support revenue goals required to sustain the business. Only after business goals were articulated could we assess how best to leverage the website architecture, directories, data, graphical interface, crawl-ability of public pages, optimization of assets, naming conventions for database-driven content, geo-location, marketing, and conversion mechanisms to support those goals.

After a thorough analysis, I identified the website's ability to compete in search, deliver value, and promote conversion through membership, sharing, event registration, etc. We were able to identify how they inadvertently overlooked some of the value inherent to these assets and chart a path to optimize them to improve member experience and search on the site and on search engines.

Because we took the time to align the website with the business, we were able to significantly increase the website's visibility, clicks, and conversion in major cities across North America. We showed them how to duplicate the methods we deployed for them and implemented for them a daily method to continue expanding their reach, membership base, and market share.

Before you think all that is needed to offset this scenario is a website designer, read the next example.

Real-World Insight: *Consumer Brand*

One company became a client after its president heard me speak at an annual industry leadership conference. He invited me to work with his team redesigning their website.

Upon review, I was shocked to find the website of this multi-national brand could not be found in the top 15 pages of search on any search engine. If you know anything about search, it is that if your website does not appear in the top five results of page 1 search results, your brand's ability to compete in the consumer space is greatly diminished.

What they desperately needed was help getting out of their own way. They hired a world-class agency to build their website, which just happened to be the same agency that created the website that did not perform in search. This would be no small task.

The portfolio of the agency was, and remains, quite prestigious. One would expect best practices and performance-driven process to be the engine behind the beautiful designs they created for household brands. Do not let this fool you. Having discussed this with others, agencies are often very slow to adopt best practices simply because it diminishes their potential for billings. I know this sounds cynical. However, as a marketer, I instinctively approach the website like any other business asset.

Their website featured Flash on the home page, hover navigation, and practically no text or mechanisms to contact the company. After great expense and effort, the client ended up with a website that was very pretty, but did nothing to engage the visitor. The website had essentially become a movie trailer, a teaser of things to come. Unfortunately, because consumers want to be able to research, compare, and purchase, this website was destined to disappoint everyone but the agency.

The Flash website had no content, so the website was not search engine friendly. Additionally, Google could not "preview" Flash sites from search results, which also put the site at a disadvantage. Then there was the topic of mobile. As the iPhone entered the market as the primary mobile device, this website became less visible with every visitor that came to the site on the iOS (Apple Operating System) because mobile devices do not support Flash. For this client, mobile visitors would be among the most qualified and easy to convert. Failure to serve an experience to these visitors literally translated to lost sales. It took two years for this company to acknowledge the need to address the needs of their growing mobile audience.

Lessons Learned

Mobile usage continues to grow exponentially—Consumers increasingly choose smartphones and tablets over PCs and laptops. The number of website visits from mobile devices is expected to exceed those by desktops by the end of 2012, or shortly thereafter, making mobile an important consideration. This is why the chapter on Mobile precedes website design and website build-out.

Organizations that rely upon their designers to create a user experience often find themselves in similar situations. Once they get past being shocked and angered with their vendor for not explaining the impact of the decisions they were presented with, they understand how important it is to lead the discussion and leverage business objectives to make informed decisions.

Handing over the website to a vendor without doing the proper preparation can be quite costly. A proactive approach can greatly improve the chances your website will deliver what you envisioned when you first made the decision to build or redesign a website. I provide you with the information you need to clearly articulate your requirements, know what questions to ask to identify where they may need assistance, and provide the "secret sauce" that only your organization can provide.

The process and information I provide in this book is designed to enable you to take a similar approach and improve the performance of your website.

2. *Investing in a Website Not Optimized for Search*

Search is a top daily activity for Internet users of all ages. Internet users search as often as they use email (Pew Research Center, 2012).

This makes investing in search a no-brainer for those selling to consumers. Brands that focus on selling to companies often challenge how valuable search is to their business. "Our customers are not searching for our products or services" is a phrase I am surprised to hear. When I ask those who utter these words, "What is the first thing you do when you are seeking a solution to a problem?" they always say, "Search." Because consumers are also professionals responsible for making business-purchase decisions, search is just as important for a B2B (business to business) brand as it is for a B2C (business to consumer) brand.

Search should be the leading source of traffic for most websites. If your business will rely upon search engine visibility to reach new customers and generate revenue, search engine optimization will require experience to be truly effective, especially in today's quickly changing search engine environment. The web elite know that a well-optimized website can reduce or eliminate dependence upon paid search and advertisement as a primary source of traffic. Reducing the cost of website traffic directly reduces the cost of acquisition of new customers, even when factoring in the upfront cost of SEO.

Most organizations expect a new website to be optimized. This expectation is amplified when the agency, designer, or firm claims expertise in SEO. However, more times than not, even if optimization is discussed prior to beginning the project, SEO is not included in website services. Believe it or not, this scenario has become far too common among highly visible, seemingly successful web companies that appear to be well qualified. This is just one of the scenarios I have witnessed time and again over the years that compelled me to write this book. Far too many companies invest in a new website assuming SEO would automatically be included in the website.

Search engines don't "see" your website the same way humans do as a visual experience. They seek data. SEO experts include factors such as text-to-code ratio, content above the fold, load time, organization of content, and links between pages and posts when optimizing a website. No design should be approved without a careful review by someone who has mastered the search landscape over many years.

Consciously deciding to build a website that is not capable of performing in search is a path I hope you would reconsider after reading this book. Investing in a website that you believed to include SEO, only to find out later that it is not, is a common, costly error that is preventable.

As I mention more than once in this book, most organizations get exactly what they asked for when they hire a website firm or allocate in-house resources to build a website. Problems arise when perception meets reality. Countless businesses every year invest significant resources in the design, development, and launch of their websites. Some will include SEO. Unfortunately, just as the website is about to go live, many will learn that the website was not optimized for search. These brands and businesses are forced to face an 11th-hour decision: choose between going live, knowing it will not deliberately compete in search, or put the project back into the production schedule and absorb additional cost to search engine optimize the website.

I cannot defend the web design and development companies that deliberately sell a website to their clients absorbing every last dime of that budget before illuminating the fact that the website is not optimized for search. What I intend to do, however, is prevent you from making this critical mistake.

The responsibility to make sure search is part of the website plan rests squarely on the shoulders of the "client." Far too many companies did not specifically address SEO when they signed the dotted line for the agreement. So, they got exactly what they asked for—no SEO.

SEO is not an add-on, or post-production process. SEO should be part of website architecture, design, development, copy writing, mobile, and usability processes, as outlined in subsequent chapters.

3. *Defining the Website with Budget*

I cannot stress this enough. Cost does not dictate how well your website will perform. There are plenty of very expensive websites that cannot be found in the top 25 pages of Google or convert a visitor to a customer, and plenty of inexpensive websites that can be found in the highly coveted #1, #2, and #3 positions in search.

A winning website is in the eye of the beholder; because of this, advertising agencies and design firms are among the most well-compensated website creators even though many of these organizations fail to apply best practices in website design, usability, content, SEO and conversion. Instead, they often center their goal around their core strength: creative design, cool technology, a template, or dependence on paid search for traffic. When you depend on their guidance to build the website, the site will be constructed to achieve profitability—for them. Because requirements directly impact budget, it is incumbent upon you to define what will create profitability for your brand.

For example, I was hired by a large corporation to provide SEO for a new website. Their previous website could not be found in Google's top 20 pages. Because few people even click beyond page 1, this website was essentially invisible to new customers. It was my responsibility to enable the client to make informed decisions that would lead to the creation of a website that would support their goals.

The agency was pushing hard to create a Flash website. Adobe Flash was not search engine friendly, or mobile friendly at the time. You see, the agency wanted to create what was familiar to them, what would enhance their portfolio, and what would be worthy of substantial fees. The focus was on what the agency wanted to provide the client, rather than providing the best possible user experience for consumers and delivering results for the client. The client fell in love with the bells and whistles of the design and disregarded recommendations that would promote performance in search, usability, and conversion. As a result, they were forced to invest much more money to correct the problems they created for themselves by not adhering to best practices on the front end.

The beauty of the Internet is that it is based upon data. When I advise clients, my recommendations are not based on my personal preferences, but industry best practices, data, guidance from search engines, testing, and monitoring over many years. The methodology I have developed over the years is similar to my peers. I continually adapt to maintain and improve performance of the many aspects of a website that impact search engine performance. I expect you to view the website the same way by the time you complete this book.

4. *Treating the Website as a Project*

To most, the website is a project, but entering into the "project" mindset is a fatal flaw that has led to the demise of far too many websites and the organizations they were created to support. Unfortunately, brands have been conditioned to take this approach, which is exactly why most websites fail. I will demonstrate why you—and those you hire—must not view the website as a project.

The Website as a Commodity

Over the years, so much emphasis has been placed on the website as a static object. Even Wikipedia defines the website as a "set of pages." Yet, it must be so much more if it is to be of any value. Dialogue has reduced the website to this idea of it as a fixed entity, which has led web-service providers to create packages and templates they can sell in volume. In-house teams typically approach the website as a project with a definitive timeline and deliverables. As a result, those seeking website services have been conditioned to shop for, purchase, and invest in websites as projects with pre-defined scopes of pages, hours invested, objects, or features. The continued perception of the website as an object has continually reduced the perceived value of the website, which directly translates to how much time, energy, and resources a brand is willing to invest in a website. Interestingly, brands expect more than ever from the website.

All Too Familiar

For anyone who has worked in the industry or been a consumer of web services long enough, the above scenario is far too familiar. I have discussed this with numerous other experts in the industry and we all agree. Misinformation and perceptions like these stand in the way of organizations being successful online. Most of us experts share the common belief that the more educated and informed a client is, the easier it is to help them achieve their goals. There a few, though, who have chosen to prey on those with little knowledge. The websites they churn out deliver the barest minimum and cost more than they are worth. Let's put them out of business, shall we?

Resist the Project Mentality

Remember that the typical website vendor views the website as a project with a beginning, middle, and an end. Because the project scope will directly impact resource allocation and profitability for the team or vendor responsible for the website, you must accept that their goals will not be the same as your goals. For this reason, deferring the website vision, strategy, KPIs, etc. to the website team or vendor responsible for creating the website is where many organizations make their single greatest mistake.

There are always exceptions. However, despite perception, much of the web industry is built upon the minimization of the business in exchange for focus on the project.

Different Goals

Once the website team deems the project complete, they move on to the next project—mission accomplished. They have fulfilled their role and will move on to other responsibilities or projects.

Conversely, at the very moment that the website is deemed complete and goes live, the role the website was designed to fill has only just begun. Until that moment, the website was an expense for the organization it was built for. Only after the website goes live, can it begin to fulfill its destiny as an asset.

These goals—those of the website team and those of the organization—do not reconcile unless the organization invests the proper time and energy in owning the website, and at the very moment the web team completes the task of building the website, is fully prepared to take responsibility for the success of the website.

I share with you a framework, based on the process I have used over and again, to enable you to take control of the website as a vital business asset.

5. *Choosing a Random Domain (URL) for Your Website.*

What's in a name? For a website, a great deal. The domain, or URL by which your website is identified, resides among billions of other pages and posts on the web. The "address" you give your website is extremely important. Choosing your domain, adding a domain, or replacing a domain should be done with ample understanding of marketing, cultural, and search engine implications.

Your domain will bring visitors to your website's "front door." It will also appear on your business card, marketing collateral, social media profile, and whenever it is mentioned by the media, competitors, customers, and reviewers. A domain should clearly reflect your brand. Acronyms should be avoided unless that is how your organization is known. You can also register a primary domain for the website, as well as other domains featuring the product you are known best for. For example, "Kindle" is the name of Amazon's own e-book tablet reader. If a consumer enters Kindle.com into a search bar, it automatically directs consumers to a page dedicated to Kindles on Amazon.com. We will talk about the value of landing pages in the SEO and Content chapters.

Choosing a Domain

There are a number of TLD (top level domains) from which to choose. Some domains are open (such as .com, .biz, .info, .net, .org). Some domains require authentication (.museum, .aero, .pro, and .travel).

The following are some considerations if you decide to register a new domain for your website.

Because people will respond to marketing material and return to your domain after visiting once, try to make it logical and simple.

Refrain from creative acronyms. Use brand and/or keywords in your domain when legally appropriate and available.

Reflecting your brand is always desirable when choosing a domain. If you are a small business in a competitive local market and are more likely to get more business via *what* you are rather than *who* you are, choosing a domain with keywords in it can be beneficial because people sometimes guess URLs rather than search for them. Plus, search engines have been known to include domain (and URLs) in search algorithms. A couple of examples might be Gino's East Pizza (FABulous pizza by the way!) vs. Chicago Style Pizza, or Bahamas scuba lessons vs. the name of a local shop. Choose which works best for your brand.

.com remains the primary domain for business and commerce brands and is typically most easily remembered by customers.

Some domains are specific to the United States (.us, .edu, .gov, .mil).

Country code top-level domains may require a physical presence or verification.

.tv is an up-and-coming, American top-level domain for video and web television.

There are many more to choose from based on the type of organization you have, the geographic market in which you operate, and your goals. Most domains cost between $9 and $39, depending on which registrar you choose. All domains are created equal as long as you purchase it from an authorized ICANN domain registrar. There is always the chance that someone may have purchased a domain that you want to register; these speculators purchase domains with the hope that someone, someday will want to buy it. Domain squatting can pay off as .com domains dwindle, but I have found that there are still plenty of .com domains to be registered if you are creative enough and/or have a unique brand.

A number of new generic top level domains (gTLDs) are likely to appear, according to applicants responding to ICANN's invitation to request a new top level domain. Those who have submitted requests include .aaa by the American Automobile Association, Inc., .apple by Apple Inc., .hotel which was requested by multiple applicants, and .weather which was applied for by The Weather Channel LLC.

Because the application costs $185,000 (yes, you read that right), you will want to carefully consider whether this path is right for your brand before you consider applying for a top-level domain.

Domain longevity, especially in the context of its relationship with a website and its content, is important to SEO. A website with a brand-spanking new domain can expect to face a bit of an uphill battle when competing in search against a competitor with a domain that is years old. However, I've been able to assist companies with new domains get to the top of Google in short periods of time, so it most certainly can be done.

Changing a Domain

This should be done only when necessary, and with great caution. A domain change doesn't just affect the home page of the website, it affects every page and post that resides on that domain. Unless managed properly, a domain change can be detrimental to the health of your brand and SEO. Google encourages keeping all content under one domain, which makes perfect sense for planning and ongoing management perspective.

If you are tempted to create mini-sites, stand-alone landing pages, or micro-sites, you may consider creating those pages within the confines of your primary domain, registering a domain for those pages, and referring it to the pages. Try not to mask, as domain masking makes it more difficult for others to share content pages in social media or email and for search engines to identify landing pages.

Cloaking is considered high-risk behavior from a search perspective. Cloaking is when you make one set of data available to website users and to Googlebot and it goes against Google's Quality Guidelines. Matt Cutts says there is no such thing as "white hat" cloaking. However, delivering geolocation and mobile versions of that data by IP address is not considered cloaking. Learn more about this topic, visit MillionDollarWebsite.TV for a link to this video featuring Google's Matt Cutts.

6. *Starting with the Design of the Website*

Never, never, never (did I say *never*?) begin the website process with design. This will make perfect sense to you as we travel through the logical process of website mission, strategy, planning, architecture, usability, content, and optimization. A website based purely on design is destined to fail most organizations.

7. *Defining Website by Number of "Pages"*

There is no way to realistically determine how many pages your website will require until you have defined what the website will offer visitors and what the intended outcome will be.

Forcing websites to fit a ready-made or pre-determined outline or package may be okay if you have a plan to launch a simple landing page or microsite. However, this will not serve the needs of most organizations. A website should be built to meet the needs of customers while supporting business goals. This can rarely be achieved with a one-, two-, five-, or ten-page template website.

Often web-based programs, like those offered by domain registrars and hosting companies, offer hosted website packages based on a number of pages. As tempting as the low cost may be, never build a website in this context until you have performed due diligence. With a low-cost website, strategy, mission, and requirements are just as important—if not more important—because of how much you must achieve with less. Being prepared to leverage a low-cost or custom website to achieve your goals requires similar thought and process applied to large-budget websites.

8. Treating the Website as a Marketing Expense

Unlike a brochure, catalogue, direct mail, advertising, or media campaign, the website is not an expense—it is a business asset. Uniquely capable of interacting with customers in real-time, the website deserves as much attention as you give hiring salespeople, customer service representatives, marketing professionals, managers, and support staff.

Contrary to what most of the business community has been led to believe, the website is not a one-time investment. Regardless of how much it will cost, appropriate resources must be allocated before, during, and after site launch in order to realize return on investment. Demonstrating that you are in tune with your industry, customers, and competitors is imperative to competing in today's digital marketplace. The website is the predominant voice for your brand, responsible for educating customers, differentiating from competitors, and initiating a relationship with customers. I show you how to leverage content to support your strategy while appeasing the appetite of customers and search engines throughout the book so that you will be fully prepared to adopt the website as a part of business operations and overall success.

9. Forgetting That Customers Are in Control

As technology advances, expectations of website visitors continually grow. Visitors want to be in control of their online experience. Each visitor brings a slightly different perspective to the user experience. The more control you offer to visitors, the more memorable your website will be. The more memorable your website is, the more your brand remains "front of mind" for visitors. They will be more likely to share their impression and experience with those they influence and, by doing so, influence purchase decisions.

Putting visitors in the driver's seat is an important part of the website planning process. Before you plan design or content, you must have a plan for meeting the needs of your customers. In the chapter on "Who Do You Love," I show you how to leverage personas to meet the needs of your visitors with paths to conversion and engagement.

10.   *Failing to Create a Memorable Moment*

The Internet is an interactive, multi-sensory platform, an environment where people can read, listen to, click, and interact with your content. The more opportunities you offer that promote the engagement of visitors, the better, more stimulating, and memorable your website will be.

A simple, fun example of interactivity is a Google Doodle featuring the characters of the original Star Trek to celebrate the brand's 46th anniversary. The Doodle featured an interactive graphic with background sound akin to the "bridge" on the starship Enterprise and enabled users to click their way through three scenes. View a video of the entire Star Trek Google Doodle on YouTube.

This fun example sparks the imagination. And, although your website may not call for a fun feature, you would be well served to consider creating a memorable way for visitors to consume your content and interact with your brand. What is memorable will vary greatly. For example, a manufacturing brand that offers a video that demonstrates how to use a new product in an unexpected or entertaining way could go viral if resellers, retailers, and customers find it engaging. Making an impression is an invaluable use of the website for brands in any industry.

11.   *Overlooking the Fact That Quality Counts*

Despite perception, "quality" is no longer subjective when it comes to evaluating a website.

Google, Bing, and Yahoo share quality guidelines for websites that reflect best practices that go beyond what most believe to impact search. These guidelines resonate with the methods embraced, endorsed, and put into practice by the web elite. However, quality guidelines elude most in the web industry.

With only seconds to engage the visitor when visitors arrive, navigation to key content, regardless of what page they land on, is vital to success. Design must promote usability and adapt to the device the visitor is using. Too little or too much content is detrimental. A website with little to no "data" (content) works much harder to compete in search. I expand on the importance of data in the chapter on SEO. Visitors decide how much or how little of the website they will consume, so the website experience must support your goals on its own merit, enabling visitors to find the nuggets that lead them along the path to becoming customers.

12.   *Copying the Website of a Competitor*

This is a tempting shortcut for some, but it is always a mistake that never works. Here's why:

Some think that copying another website's content and/or metadata will help them achieve equal footing in search engines. Today's search algorithms are so sophisticated that not only will this never happen, it will likely backfire.

Google has always frowned upon duplicate content, and recent algorithm updates now punish websites that duplicate content. Website content is copyrighted material, so you are essentially stealing unless you are given license or permission to publish content owned by someone else. In addition to the written narrative, copyrighted works include websites filled with product from a database that others share, or retail websites using manufacturer descriptions to sell product. We discuss this further in the chapter on Content, but for now let's just say ANY page or post featuring content that appears anywhere else on the web, especially if it was published there first, is essentially invisible to search engines, making your presentation of that content invisible to your target audiences via search.

Copying metadata from another website never works. Why? Because metadata is only a fraction of what search engines use to determine what appears in SRPs (search engine result pages). Metadata must be uniquely written to reflect what is on each page or post. The mere fact that your content resides on a separate domain within code unique to your website automatically eliminates exact duplication.

Google is extremely smart, and getting smarter every day. In summer 2012 Google announced that the search algorithm had been updated to penalize for copyrighted works. This, combined with the Panda and Penguin updates that already penalized for duplicate content and Google's ability to identify who was the first to publish specific content, should dissuade you from attempting to leverage the success of another for your own gain.

Perhaps you are thinking about duplicating or emulating the design of a competitor's website. Unless your one and only goal is to knock off the brand of a competitor, this will not work either—nor should you want it to.

Your brand is unique and likely better than your competitor in some way. The key to competing on the web is to capture the attention of customers and win their business using that unique differentiator. You cannot differentiate your brand from competitors and help customers appreciate what makes your brand or offering worthy of their business if there is no discernible difference between you. You are doing your brand and your customers a disservice by failing to help them make an informed decision. Not to mention, what happens if that competitive brand falls out of favor because of a product failure, publicity nightmare, or bad reviews? You don't want your brand to go down with their ship, do you? There are ways to benefit from the "best of" your competitors' online experiences without giving up the individuality that will put your website on the path to success.

There really are no short cuts to creating a winning website. Sure, you could just throw something together and hope for the best. However, if you really want to go head-to-head with a competitor and achieve your goals, the process I outline in this book will help you do so in a highly deliberate and proactive manner.

13. *Writing Content before the Website Design is Planned and Developed*

Chances are you are beginning to get a feel for what it will take to create a winning website. Writing content for a website that has not been properly planned is like trying to select furniture for a room in a house to be built that does not yet have architectural plans. Building a house is a very good analogy for building a website. You wouldn't trust a college student to design and build your home (hopefully), so why would you trust one of the most valuable assets of your business to one?

14. *Licensing Software, Content, or Choosing a Web Platform before Defining Your Own Requirements*

One of the most important decisions you will make is what platform your website is on. Do not leave this decision to your team or vendors. Where you choose to build your website will directly impact your website's performance and success.

Custom development is highly desirable but most often cost prohibitive for small businesses, medium-sized enterprises, and start-ups. Unless the website itself is a custom application or platform like accounting software, a retail distribution model (think Amazon), financial institution, social network, or some other highly complex, regulated, or proprietary platform, you will find that open source and CMS (content management systems) have become quite sophisticated and are able to serve the needs of nearly any brand.

Proprietary CMS, once the crown jewel in web development, can be attractive. Back in the early days of the Internet, organizations had to pay for custom development if they wanted to offer features like shopping carts, catalogs, downloads of content, etc. CMS became the only cost-effective alternative for most brands. The development for one became available to many, helping the developers offset the cost of creating custom applications so the first client that needed it didn't have to bear the entire cost for a feature others were asking for or were likely to need. This is where many industry-specific web systems still live. Companies that specialize in websites for accountants, attorneys, car dealerships, etc. continue to use the proprietary CMS model today.

One of the downsides of a proprietary CMS is that you will be tied to that company, agency, designer, or developer for the life of the website, even if you terminate your relationship with them. Think you can take your code and go elsewhere? Think again. When you license a website from these firms, you own only your content (and sometimes not even content if you do not designate such in your agreement); you do not own your website code. This can be problematic if, once your website matures, you wish to deviate from the norm or want more or different features to improve the performance of your website. You will be limited by what they offer or forced to start from scratch. Because adoption and integration of features that leverage the latest in best practices typically take longer for those who build proprietary CMS systems to integrate, make sure you fully understand your goals and how well the solution will support them now and in the future before making the decision to go this direction.

Open Source platforms are free, and it has become one of the most attractive and affordable platforms for website development, making Open Source a dominant player in the website industry. WordPress, Joomla, and Drupal are among the mainstream Open Source platforms most attractive to organizations seeking high levels of functionality at a reasonable cost. In July 2012, WordPress was powering over 54 million websites. Organizations as large as CNN, NBC Sports, UPS, TechCrunch, TED, and the National Football League (NFL), and as small as your local entrepreneur (and even yours truly), use WordPress as their website platform.

However, Open Source doesn't mean generic or cheap. Website theme, design, graphics, content, and SEO for a winning website will still require an investment in time and resources. In fact, many who sell "custom" website design use Open Source platforms, including agencies, design firms, and development firms.

The attraction of Open Source is that the development community is continually solving problems, adapting to best practices, and making administration of the website easier. Plug-ins are like the apps you find in Google Play or the Apple Store. Each outlines features, what version of the platform they are compatible with, and includes reviews by other users. Most are free, but a few require a purchase. Many request donations as a reward for their work and to enable them to continue development to meet the ever-changing needs of the community.

A word of caution: When your designer or programmer begins creating custom applications or plug-ins for an Open Source platform, you immediately shift from the Open Source to the proprietary CMS category for the simple reason that you are no longer able to update as new versions are released and integrate new plug-ins as they become available. Doing so often "breaks" the custom code. You will want to maintain the integrity of the platform if you wish to continually integrate some of the fastest and most sophisticated features on the Internet into your website. We cover how to navigate the customization of Open Source for best results later in the book, and I offer you guidelines and tips on how to choose the platform that will best support your goals in the chapter on Platform and Tools.

15.   *Planning to Search Engine Optimize the Website After Website Goes Live*

What a common and huge mistake this is. SEO must be an essential part of the DNA of your website. You cannot introduce SEO after a website is complete and expect the same results you would get from a website built to perform in search.

In 2009 I spoke about this very subject at Web 2.0 in San Francisco. The room was packed for all SEO sessions. So, after many had listened to Black Hat SEOs reveal all the ways to trick Google and search engines into displaying a website at the top of the SRPs, I was talking White Hat SEO that began with planning, architecture, design, metadata, and content. All 500 seats were filled, and there were people sitting on the floor, standing in the back, and spilling out into the hallway. I stressed, over and again, how vital it was to integrate SEO into the entire website process. At the end of the process, as attendees representing organizations around the world (including the big search engines) lined up to say hello, request a copy of my presentation, and discuss engagement, I was told over again how the perspective I offered would help them change the way their organization approached search. Of course, this was extremely gratifying. One never knows who is going to be in the room or how the presentation might be accepted when you veer from the hype.

I am here to tell you the very same. SEO must play a role in website architecture, design, content, and even in the details of naming conventions for files, products, URLs, blog posts, images, etc. A website optimized after the fact is better than not optimized at all. However, if you are going to invest in SEO, why wouldn't you want to gain the full benefit from your investment?

I walk you through the entire SEO framework in the SEO chapter so that you may approach website SEO the way top-tier SEO experts do.

16.   *Sending Out Vague Website RFPs*

If an RFP is not accompanied by extremely specific requirements—including strategy, site map, brand direction, clearly defined goals, and an outline of KPIs and conversion for each customer type—then there is no way to conduct an "apples to apples" comparison of proposals when choosing a website vendor for part or all of your website.

RFP Perspectives

Each vendor you invite to submit a proposal has built their business around their specific talent, experience, and expertise. Their proposal will integrate methods and preferences that work best and deliver profitability for them. I've witnessed this from all sides. I've been among those writing the RFP, writing proposals in response to RFPs, and frequently advising clients during the review of RFPs to select a vendor.

Unfortunately, most organizations do not know how to write a website RFP that will deliver exactly what they need. Vendors care less about what you are asking for than how they can provide it at a price that will win them the contract and still deliver a healthy profit margin, or that will enable them to use the account to land other clients that will be more profitable. The result is rarely positive. Proposals often omit or totally disregard what the RFP has requested. This should automatically disqualify that vendor. If they cannot follow your direction when outlining your request, whatever would make you think they will be responsive to your needs and requirements throughout the rest of the website process?

Experience Counts

Unfortunately, many who submit RFPs and review the proposals responding to the RFP are responsible for creating a website only every couple, three, or even five years.

Because the Internet changes so quickly, the client is already at a distinct disadvantage and is often forced to trust that the proposal includes everything requested the way they envisioned it, even if they could not articulate it fully. This is often a fatal mistake that can be costly and sometimes lead to the demise of the company.

Later on, we walk through best practices for preparing an RFP and guidelines you can use to make the RFP process work better and produce higher quality responses that will enable your organization to make a truly informed decision about who is best suited to deliver the solution that will yield the best results.

17. *Not Including Mobile in Your Website Plan*

Your website's performance on mobile is no longer an option. With mobile devices expected to outperform desktops for Internet activity, it is imperative that your website either render efficiently on mobile devices or that you create an alternative user experience on a dedicated mobile site or mobile app.

73 percent say that they've encountered a website that was too slow to load on a mobile device.

51 percent of mobile Internet users visited a website that crashed, froze, or resulted in an error.

38 percent of mobile users have encountered a website that was not available to view on the mobile device.

75 percent said they would be less likely to return to a website they couldn't visit via mobile (KISSmetrics, 2012).

It is very likely that you actively use mobile frequently to find information. So, why would your customers be any different? I have heard just about every reason imaginable from organizations that do not believe they have enough mobile visitors to warrant consideration. Is losing one ideal customer for life a compelling reason to consider mobile? One visit is all it takes to lose a customer forever.

Mobile access to search and websites is on the rise and expected to grow exponentially in the coming years. You should plan your website accordingly. We cover best practices in the chapter on Mobile. At this point I simply want to ensure that you understand how important mobile is to every website, regardless of industry.

18.   *Replacing an Old Website with a New Website without Proper Attention to SEO*

I cannot stress this enough. Far too many times to mention, brands create a new website that literally unravels everything they were doing right with their previous website. A website redesign or a move to a new platform can be disastrous when you do not proactively manage SEO. Search engines are intimately familiar with every aspect of your website. When you change factors like design, CMS, content, metadata, or conversion mechanisms, it inherently modifies the many aspects that contribute to search rank.

I recently visited the website of a client we had worked very hard with a couple years back to achieve #1, #2, and #3 positions in Google for just about any keyword phrase their target customers were using. They declined support after the website went live as they went on to reap the rewards of their investment. Then they moved the website from one e-commerce platform to another and completely wiped out every little bit of optimization performed on the website, including unique product descriptions. As a result, the website is nowhere to be found on Google—the primary source of their traffic and sales. After a considerable investment of time and money, someone in the organization made a decision they believed to be an improvement that proved instead to be devastating to the bottom line.

19.   *Relying upon Web Professionals to Create the Website Strategy*

No one understands your business and goals better than you do. No one cares about results more than you do. Although convenient, deferring to an agency, website design firm, or programmer to build your website without first setting key parameters can be a very costly mistake.

I'm not suggesting that professionals at agencies, programmers, design and new media firms cannot add value to this process. They absolutely can and you should leverage their expertise to improve every aspect of the website experience. What I am suggesting, however, is that you take ownership of the website and lead the charge to create the environment on which your organization will depend upon for the next one, two, three or more years.

We delve into specifics on what exactly you should do before sitting down to launch a website project in-house or with vendors throughout the book. The most important takeaway at this point is that you and your organization must master the website. I guess I'm asking you to give new meaning to the term "webmaster".

20.   *Building a Website That Does Not Have Your "Ideal Customer" in Mind*

Your website is consumed one visitor at a time. This vital aspect to how the web works is often overlooked. Websites are built to push messaging, information, and to request a sale, yet few take into account the mere fact that each unique visitor is a human, just like you.

Not every human is qualified to be a customer for your brand. And, even some of those who may meet basic qualifications won't be good customers. Targeting is key.

Your website should attract ideal customers and deliver a quality experience. It all begins by pre-qualifying the click through SEO and promoting usability and access to content in a user experience that appeals to each of your customers, one visitor at a time.

In chapter 6; "Who Do You Love?" we explore how to leverage customer personas to drive website strategy, design, content, SEO, and conversion.

21.   *Not Being Prepared to Begin Maintaining the Website the Day It Goes Live*

On the very day the website project ends for the team that created it, the website comes to life for the brand. The web elite know that work has only just begun when the website goes live. No organization likes hearing this after investing time, money, and resources into creating the website. Plus, they typically have not been prepared for this reality because the initial goal was to get the website budget approved.

Ongoing analysis, optimization, promotion, and maintenance are as important to the website as the investment made to bring the site to life.

22.   *Neglecting Kernels of Wisdom Provided by Website Analytics and Other Historic Data to Guide the Mapping of the New Website Strategy*

You can't chart a path forward until you know where you are. A website is a vehicle that your business can use to reach your destination. Before you modify, improve, or replace an existing website, you must consider the historical relationship between your brand and your customers. This insight can be accessed through website analytics form submissions, opt-ins, conversions, and other important data.

Every aspect of your user experience either improves or diminishes the quality of engagement with website visitors. If one of the most important pages of your website takes so long to load that most visitors abandon the page, you will want to correct this on your new website. If there is a video, demo, or testimonial that contributes to a higher conversion rate, you will want to include this in the new website. These are just examples to illustrate how important historic data is to the website planning process.

In chapter 5, I show you how to conduct a thorough website audit and analysis that will be invaluable in the website redesign process.

My goal is to help you become a more savvy, knowledgeable master of the website. The more you know, the better decisions you will make, and the more cost efficient and effective the website will become as a direct result of your leadership.

Chapter 4:

Top 10 Reasons to Create a New Website

When it is time to update the website you have, or build an entirely new website?

1. The website cannot perform organically in search engines.

2. The website no longer delivers leads or customers.

3. Cost of customer acquisition has escalated to exceed overall benefit.

4. Brand is losing more business to competitors.

5. Website content cannot be updated by those managing the brand.

6. There is no RSS feed.

7. The website cannot facilitate social media integration or sharing.

8. Bounce rate has exceeded 50 percent site-wide.

9. Bottom line of the business enjoys no benefit from the website.

10. Customers increasingly criticize quality of website user experience, performance, or value.

Chapter 5:

Website Planning 101

If you heed my advice in no other chapter in this book but this one, you will be ahead of the game. Of course, I want you to read and apply the information provided throughout the entire book; however, this chapter represents the single most common "missing ingredient" of nearly every website that fails to fulfill its potential—planning.

What Comes First?

Despite what others believe, you must resist the temptation to approach the website as a design vehicle or a platform to display really cool technology. The choice to feature "bright, shiny objects" may be important to the appeal and performance of a website, but it should never be introduced without good reason and proper context.

If you follow my advice and hold off on meetings to launch website design, copy writing, and application development until you can initiate those discussions in proper context with supporting documents, you will see a great difference in the focus and accuracy of these efforts. When you lead these discussions with confidence and clarity, you will save a great deal of time and money. (After all, time is money whether your website team is in-house, external, or a combination thereof.)

Before you even begin interviewing those who will be responsible for executing your vision, whether in-house, vendors, or a combination thereof, you must be prepared to articulate your website mission and strategy. Vendors can be extremely valuable, but they should not develop your strategy. The strategy should come from within your organization, regardless of its size. Even if you decide to seek the expertise of an e-business strategist, your business model, the needs of your customers, and your operations and goals must be the foundation for planning your website.

You must own the website vision—the strategy—just as you would for your business as a whole. Once you have become the master of the strategy, you will most likely need assistance in transforming that strategy into an interactive experience that will perform.

No Website before Its Time

Websites fail when they are built before they were properly incubated. For years I have heard the same desperate pleas from organizations that deployed a website before it was fully developed. "The website gets lots of visitors, but no one will buy" or "The website has a fantastic conversion rate, but the website is not attracting enough visitors" are common laments. The most painful to hear is "We don't have enough traffic to be viable" as this indicates failure to optimize the site for search, which the web elite know is vital to every website.

Some websites simply fall flat and deliver nothing but a great big headache. I can't tell you how often entrepreneurs have come to me after investing tens of thousands of dollars, some even investing their retirement money to start their dream Internet business, only to end up broke with no sales to show for their time and trouble. It wasn't because they didn't understand the business they were trying to create. They failed because they lacked ample knowledge to be the master of the website. As a result, they were easily led astray by solutions and services that benefited the providers but failed to deliver results to the owner.

You do not have to be a technical wiz or creative genius to master the website. All it takes is a deliberate approach and due diligence.

In this chapter I walk you through the website planning process. Throughout the rest of the book, I share what the web's most experienced e-business and digital strategists know and guide you through the most important decisions you can make regarding your website.

You must become the master of the website. Once you have embraced ownership of this business asset, the potential for success multiplies exponentially.

Best Practices

Best practices are much more than a list of key items, such as including a home button, contact page, address, an xml sitemap, footer, etc. Best practices encompass innumerable checks and balances that together promote seamless delivery of the website to desktops and mobile devices in an effective and efficient manner.

Why are these important? Best practices don't just work behind the scenes to make the website mechanics work better; they contribute to how well your website performs for visitors by creating an efficient, pleasurable user experience.

Because best practices also directly impact mechanical functions of the website, such as bounce rate, pages viewed, clicks, conversion, and search engine performance, many are tempted to reduce the entire website to a series of mechanical maneuvers. As the web matures, more is expected from the website from both a user and an organizational standpoint.

Even though one of Google's objectives is to deliver relevant results in search, they too have elevated their demands of websites that wish to reach new customers in search. As the search landscape has become increasingly competitive over the years, their algorithm has included more of the website in determining search rank. In addition to "connecting the dots" between relevance between search terms and your brand and website content, Google has become much more interested in the user experience you provide your visitors. In April 2012 Google stated that they will reward "Quality" websites (more on this in the SEO chapter). Organizations that want to rely upon search must deliver a well-constructed, high-performance website in addition to optimizing for search relevance.

Strive to Build a Quality Website

Getting a website out there is far less important than creating a digital extension of your business designed to deliver results. Results are generated when you meet the needs and expectations of your audiences. The *Million Dollar Website* is a business asset grounded in quality. By deploying best practices of the web elite to create the most effective businesses and brands on the Internet, you elevate the ability of your own business or brand to support your own goals.

I show you how to begin the Website Planning Process with:

- Website Mission

- Website Strategy

- KPIs

- Site Map

Once you have completed the above, the conversation can smoothly transition to topics like SEO, website design, content, mobile, data, legacy software integration, and conversion.

There are important considerations I must bring to your attention that should play into your decisions from this point forward. The website process requires a great deal of interaction between those involved, throughout every phase. A linear approach may make it easier to plan, communicate and manage the website process. However, you will likely find yourself circling back to revisit various aspects when defining website requirements that will drive subsequent communication.

The following is an outline of the Website Planning Flow. A larger image and printable version are available online on the website: MillionDollarWebsite.TV

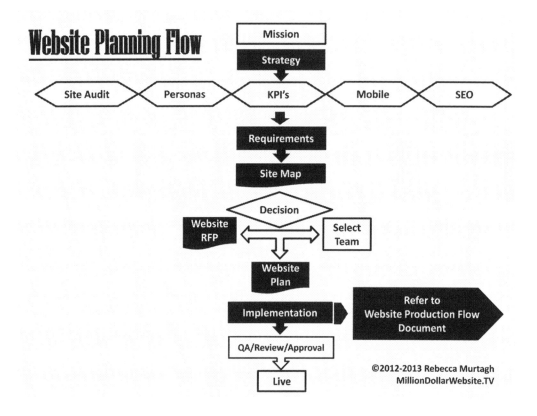

©2012-2013 Rebecca Murtagh
MillionDollarWebsite.TV

KPIs: Show Me the Money

I'm not talking here about what you will invest to build the website; I'm focusing on what you need the website to deliver.

The web elite know that no matter what your primary motivation for building a website is, money will be part of the success equation. Whether you are seeking sales, demos, members, donations, enrollments, registration, appointments, or advertisers, these goals can be defined by a transaction that relates to the exchange of money at some point.

Key Performance Indicators (KPIs) enable you to quantify the performance of the website as it relates to the bottom line. It is imperative that you define performance indicators before you move on to website strategy, design, development, optimization, etc.

Defining KPIs is the responsibility of those who will depend upon the performance of the website to meet the goals defined in the website strategy. In other words, KPIs are the responsibility of the website master. Not to be confused with calls to action or conversion mechanisms, KPIs help you quantify the effectiveness of the website and those features.

How to define KPIs

This will be unique to every organization. KPIs can be everything from completed transactions, percent of traffic coming to the website by non-branded keywords and phrases, or number of subscribers. You notice I do not say total revenue, search engine traffic, or email opt-ins. These are goals, as identified in your website strategy, and will provide insight into the direct impact the website is having on the organization. It is important your organization own and continually evaluate the website by these indicators. After all, no one will understand better than you what behaviors lead to creating a new customer. So, do not ask your vendors to provide KPIs—you must own them. Once you have defined them, you can invite your vendors to help you identify methods to measure the performance you seek to support your goals.

KPIs measure the events that lead to goal achievement, which is why you, the master of the website, must identify these performance indicators.

What actions or reactions lead to conversion of visitors to customers?

Sample KPIs for a high performance website could include:

- Number of demos requested

- Downloads of a free sample or offer

- Search for local retailers on the website

- Enrollments in rewards program

- Number of 5-star reviews on third-party website

- Number of active affiliates

- On-site advertisers

- Crowd-funding investors

- Special offer downloads or posting of tips on Foursquare

- Downloads of a comparison guide or shopping tips

As you can see, not all performance indicators are measured by the website. However, each can be attributed to what the website invites visitors to do.

Let me use an example to illustrate. The reviews on a third-party website may be vital to your business if you are in the travel, hospitality, or tourism business. Websites like Tripadvsior.com, Yelp.com, Fodors.com, Travelocity.com, Kayak.com, Priceline.com, etc. include customer reviews. Those with the most reviews with the highest rating automatically appear, or can be selected by user filters on the site. If your goal is to be in the top three for your destination, this would be a key performance indicator for your website—not because your *website* depends on these reviews, but rather because the *success of your business* does. This becomes a KPI for the website because it will be incumbent upon your website to provide all the information needed by customers to choose your property over the others.

We discuss this later, but I want to mention now that it is always important to maintain your website as the primary authority on your brand. Facebook is not your friend, and Pinterest, LinkedIn, and Twitter are not destinations. Your website should always be the preferred destination for brand, information, best offers, and ease of purchase. In the chapter on Social Media, we touch on how to properly manage the relationship between social media and your website. However, for now it is important to stress that it is imperative that the website be used to proactively connect directly with customers. Furthering one-to-one interaction and promoting conversion with your customers on the platform you own is almost always the most desirable and profitable scenario.

This will be different for every organization. If you are in the software business, one of your KPIs may be the number of demos requested. This was the primary goal of one of the technology companies I worked with. When they shared with me that they had nearly an 80-percent closer rate when they could get a customer to a live demo, the number of demo requests became a key performance indicator. Based upon this, we built a user experience that deliberately presented content and mechanisms designed to pre-qualify the customer and lead them to do what? Request the demo!

Hopefully you can adapt the principles behind the scenarios I provide to identify the KPIs for your website.

(I've also provided a simple worksheet to assist you in identifying KPIs on MillionDollarWebsite.TV)

Previous KPIs

If your old website was built with a specific outline of KPIs, now is a good time to revisit them. Determine which remain relevant, and identify any new indicators and capture them. Identifying what your website may have inherently done well and what will support new KPIs should be introduced to the new website, so be sure to capture them. You will likely want to track and compare old KPIs with new KPIs.

Updating KPIs

When you expect the website to support your goals over time (and you should), you will want to revisit these indicators any time your organization introduces a new product, service, or campaign, even if they are not introduced to the website. It is inevitable that the actions and reactions that occur between your brand and your customers on your website will reflect the effectiveness of any marketing effort—be they SEO, email campaigns, trade show promotions, or direct mail or television campaigns.

The Website Audit

Now that you have defined the objectives of the future website, you will want to leverage the features and content on your previous website that support these goals by completing a comprehensive audit of the website. This is easier said than done. You must be able to evaluate your website objectively using criteria accepted as best practices. If you are not confident in your ability to assess your website, you may find an objective analysis from an expert worthy of the investment.

Evaluation without context is worthless.

By this I mean you must know what is expected of the website before you can measure how well it delivers.

You will want to evaluate how well the website adheres to best practices and industry standards. These are not nebulous evaluations. A website's performance can be measured by general and specific thresholds.

You may never have viewed your website from this perspective. However, it is as important for your website to adhere to global best practices as it is for it to meet customer expectations for your industry.

Industry specific thresholds will be determined by none other than your customers and what they expect from you and your competitors. This immediately places your competitors on a level-playing field. How well does your website meet the expectations of your visitors?

Think about it—when you visit a website for a restaurant, there are things you expect to see, right? Menu, hours, directions, phone number, perhaps even reviews, online reservations, a contact for private parties, or integration with a third-party reservation system like OpenTable. The same is true for your website in your industry. The threshold lies with the content and features that must be included in order for your website to compete.

Embracing Industry Best Practices

We get into this in greater depth in the Content and Conversion chapters, but for the purposes of auditing your website, list the features that are "must have," "nice to have," and identify anything that you offer that your competitors have done. This is important. If you still do not have something unique to offer, or if you do not do something better than your competitors after completing the strategy of your website, you must consider why your customer will choose you over the competition. Once you have created the list, compare, with as much scrutiny as possible, how well you deliver information or features compared to your competitors. This will contribute to your USP (unique selling proposition) and will come into play when it comes to planning content and conversion for the website.

Whether you are the master of a large e-commerce, enterprise site, or the proud owner of a small business website, do not panic. These factors are easily measured and can be improved with minor adjustments. The most important take-away from this exercise is to realize that your website can, and should, meet as many of these thresholds as possible. These best practices will vary by business and industry. However, the overall picture will identify where you may need to create balance or address missing or problematic features.

I have provided a sample site audit checklist and some basic guidelines and resources on MillionDollarWebsite.TV to help you with this aspect of the website audit.

Which Platform Is Right for Your Organization?

It seems like just about anyone will build a website for a fee these days. Some will even offer to build a free website for you. Many will muster up the courage, and build their own website. Some will purchase a package from a vendor that will include a year or two of maintenance, some will create a DIY "Website Tonight" website on Go Daddy, others will choose an open source platform like WordPress, Joomla or Drupal or elect to purchase a license from Volusion, Shopify, Big Commerce, or any number of website platforms built by those specializing in video, reviews, or specific industries.

Buyer Beware.

Nothing is free. And, unfortunately, website companies are not always capable of delivering what they project.

The mere fact that a company has built dozens, hundreds, or thousands of websites does not mean they are good at what they do. In fact, some of the largest website companies and agencies that deliver website solutions do so with little to no correlation to actual performance. Many can build a website. Far fewer are qualified to deliver a website that will satisfy their clients. You want to work with those who understand how important it is for the website to actually deliver results for your organization. Even better is the professional who is willing to be accountable for what they deliver.

So, as one the millions of professionals that face the website process only once every other year, or every two or three, how can you be sure that you will end up with the website you need?

Because the same mistakes are made by so many, it may be easier to define what you want to avoid when choosing the vendor(s) or team for your website. A common denominator among the failing websites that have I have been invited to revive is that they were not planned and built in the proper context. It is not uncommon for an entire website to be built around a cool interface or multimedia introduction created by a designer. Key elements are often overlooked.

Avoid Bright, Shiny Object Syndrome

It is easy to be romanced by slick graphics, animations, and cool applications when it comes to website design. Falling in love with a bright, shiny object is an infatuation that will quickly pass once you get beneath the surface and discover that the sexy exterior had little substance in delivering return on your website investment.

Let me give you a couple of examples of how bright, shiny object syndrome can lead to trouble.

Many websites rely too heavily on Flash or content that takes time to load. Website visitors are impatient and may not wait for the site to load, or may be unable to view it at all from a mobile device. Studies show that if they have difficulty viewing or get tired of waiting for content to load, they may never return to your website. Sophisticated content may be pretty to look at and could win you (or your firm) an award, but it is not practical for most businesses or brands. So, unless you have zero plans for performance, confine Flash and heavy load-time content that is not integral to attracting new customers and converting them to customers.

Bright shiny objects are not always about the lure of design. There are occasions when a programmer or developer creates a slick new application that demonstrates code prowess that the technology community may admire, but visitors will never care about or use.

Find the Right Wow Factor

Bright shiny objects are often costly to create, and costly to remove. You can protect yourself from becoming enamored by features and function that will not support your goals by following the process I have outlined, which will produce requirements that can be used to create that "wow" factor you seek in a strategic manner that you will not regret a few months after making the investment.

You can avoid these and many other common missteps with just a little bit of thought and planning. This is exactly why I am sharing with you some of the process I have used for over 14 years to develop e-business strategy and guide the website process of clients. When you understand the entire website process and the impact of each aspect of the website, you make better decisions. This is not theory, but proven methodology.

Let's get into the natty gritty, shall we?

Chapter 6:

Who Do You Love?

One of the most overlooked factors in building a new website is the intended audience. Sounds crazy, right? You'd be shocked to know how many websites go live without considering the needs of the customer.

The web elite know it is ALL about the customers. The better you know and love them, the more valuable the user experience on the website will be.

What is a Customer?

Because I often refer to your customers throughout the book, now is a good time to define who I mean when I say "customer." It is important to realize that your website will serve more than one customer even though my experience is that most organizations initially focus on one type of customer. Actually, every organization has more than one customer type and each will arrive on the website as a visitor. Your website will appeal to people that share a specific demographic, professional level, role, geographic location, or any number of factors. And, each may approach with different expectations.

A little bit of strategic planning greatly increases the potential of a website to reach, engage, and convert website visitors to customers. I walk you through exactly how to define the user experiences that will deliver value and drive conversion.

Regardless of what industry or sector you operate in, you are likely seeking to attract more than one type of customer, including, but not limited to:

- Client/Consumer/Customer/Member/Subscriber (the obvious)

- Media

- Employee

- Investor

- Influencer

- Reviewer

- Strategic Partner

- Affiliate

- Patron/Benefactor

Which of these are your customers? Who would you add? Understanding who you are communicating with and what you intend the outcome to be will influence website design, programming, content, SEO, and conversion.

Acquisition = Conversion

How you measure the acquisition of a customer, or conversion of visitors to customers, can be measured in a variety of ways:

- Sale

- Subscription

- Demo request

- New member in a community

- Opt-in to an email list

- Media inquiry

- Employment inquiry

- Investor inquiry

We discuss conversion mechanisms in subsequent chapters. It is imperative that you identify each type of website visitor for the purposes of website strategy and planning.

You Don't Need Millions of Visitors

So how many visitors will your website need to be successful? Far too many organizations think they have to have millions of visitors to make their brand a success online. This is absolutely not true. Unless your business goals rely upon the acquisition and monetization of millions of generic visitors (like Facebook, Twitter, Amazon, etc.), the rush to get millions of visitors is the opposite of what really works in today's digital landscape.

All your website needs to do to be successful is to reach those most qualified to become your "customers" and successfully convert those visiting the website. Think about this from the perspective of mass media. If your target customers could be defined by a specific demographic, and if you could invest in mass media that would reach customers but also masses of people that would not or could not be a customer, would you? (Hopefully not!)

Unqualified visitors typically leave the site immediately, erasing any potential gain from earning that visit. Not only does this behavior dilute the overall performance metrics of the website, it also negatively affects search performance, which we will cover in the chapter on SEO.

Target, Target, Target!

The more focused you are on reaching your "ideal customers" with value, the more successful the architecture, design, SEO, content, and conversion of your website will be.

Success is measured differently for every website. Depending on your business model, success could be measured by one investor to buy your company; 100 clients enrolled in a custom-training program; 10,000 customers for a new product; or yes, even a million users on your private social network. Targeting "ideal customers" will net the best results when competing within the vast landscape of the Internet.

Target Ideal Customers

"Ideal Customers" are those you want to serve, sell to, or work for. Instead of simply targeting every small business, you may determine that small businesses owned by women and that have been open for 10 or more years are among the clients that are profitable for your business and with whom you enjoy working.

Tailoring your website to attract, serve, and sell to your "ideal customers" is one of the most effective foundations for website strategy, SEO, content, and conversion.

Personas

Personas enable you to plan the user experience for each customer type. Using personas to guide strategy ensures you are serving your customers well. Be sure to include this information when entering discussions about website architecture, design, content, usability, and conversion.

The following is a sample persona worksheet, which is also provided on the book website: MillionDollarWebsite.TV

Persona Worksheet

Insert
Persona
Image Here

Demographics

Name:

Gender:

Age (range):

Education Level:

Geographic Location:

Occupation/Role:

Affiliations:

Motivators:

Income Level:

Behavior

Internet Usage: Device Preference:

Decision Driver(s):

Level of Social Engagement:

Influenced By:

Who I Influence:

Preferred Format of Content:

Phase 1: Research

Identify the problem this customer is seeking to solve.

Phase 2: Compare

Identify how what differentiates your solution from others will resonate with this customer.

Phase 3: Purchase

What offer would you inspire this customer to choose your solution, and take action NOW?!

Persona Worksheet Provided as Supplement to Book 'Million Dollar Websites ' by Rebecca Murtagh v1a

Exercise:

Let's create a persona for an automotive dealership. To identify one of the customers we target, this sample persona represents a single professional male shopping for a new vehicle.

The next page offers an example of what that persona might look like.

A larger version is available at MillionDollarWebsite.TV

Persona Worksheet

Demographics

Name: **Ken**

Gender: **Male**

Age (range): **Late 20's**

Education Level: **Undergraduate Degree**

Geographic Location: **Northern California**

Occupation/Role: **Software Engineer**

Affiliations: **Colleagues, College Alumni, Family, Friends**
Motivators: **Technology, mechanics, power, brand, status, adventure**

Income Level: **$75,000-$90,000 / year**

Behavior

Internet Usage: **High end user, mobile dependent.**

Device Preference: **mobile, Android**

Decision Driver(s): **Finding a cool car that makes a statement about him in his new surroundings. Will seek reviews/recommendations for dealers.**

Level of Social Engagement: **Highly active.**

Influenced By: **Friends and social connections.**

Who I Influence: **Friends, Colleagues, social connections.**
Preferred Format of Content: **all relevant data including inventory, options and price, easily accessible online.**

Phase 1: Research

Best car to buy in city they he is moving to accept a new job.

Phase 2: Compare

Ample selection in model/option features, dealer reputation and proximity to his new job will be important because he is new to the area.

Phase 3: Purchase

Desired model, color & options in selected model, fair price from reputable dealer, flexible financing due to new employment.

Persona Worksheet Provided as Supplement to Book 'Million Dollar Websites ' by Rebecca Murtagh v1a

You will want to create a persona for every customer type. Once you have created the website mission (which we cover in chapter 9), I recommend revisiting these personas to ensure they align with one another.

Each persona should be a consideration throughout the planning of the website. You must determine how your website will provide value to each of them and explore all possible paths when they visit your website, appealing specifically to them through the design, content, SEO, and calls to action within those paths. You may also want to track visits, user paths, KPIs, and conversion for each customer type using Google Analytics or similar tools, which we cover in the chapter on Conversion.

Chapter 7:

_____

Goals and KPIs

The website is a major investment for any business: time, energy, collaboration, planning, execution, and of course, capital. It is important that those responsible for the website have some accountability or responsibility in the performance of it. Determine your KPIs (key performance indicators) ahead of time and articulate them clearly to every member of the team who will work on the website or who will be responsible for supporting these goals (on or offline). It is important these goals come from the brand.

Begin with the End in Mind

You must identify the end game. What do you hope to achieve?

Your strategy must artfully integrate the behavior and desires of your customers with paths to support these goals. KPIs and goals will define requirements to support the conversion of visitors representing each of personas you have created.

Identify information, functions, and actions your website must provide each customer and prioritize these functions.

List A: "must have" functions and content

List B: "nice to have" functions and content

List C: "future" additions to functions and content

Tip: Not everything you come up with may be viable this time around, but this is a great starting point for future phases or the next website. I highly recommend you capture these items, add to them over time as website performance dictates, and refer to this list when you are ready to improve or replace the website.

Are You Listening?

If you take the time to listen, your customers will tell you exactly what to deliver on your website. Invite them to take a survey. Third-party resources like ForeSee and iPerceptions are among the many who provide "Customer Satisfaction" surveys to gain insight from website visitors. If neither are feasible, closely evaluate website data in statistics and analytics programs to evaluate user entrance paths, exit paths, and conversion. This intelligence will help you serve visitors better, which should be your primary reason for existence.

Invite Collaboration

Defining the user experience is most effective when you invite contributions from representatives that interact with each of your audiences. Tap into insights from others to streamline communication or frequently requested information. For example, if customers are constantly asking how your product is different from a competitor's product, create a comparison grid. If journalists frequently request photos of your CEO, make them available on the website. If you close 90 percent of software demos, but you can't get enough people to request the demo, consider highlighting a point or two from the demo to increase demo requests. If customers frequently seek reviews of your product, feature reviews on your website. Opportunities to serve customers are endless.

Chapter 8:

The Benefits of Ownership

Believe it or not, strategy is one of the most overlooked aspects of planning a website, hands down. Over the years, I have witnessed far too many organizations dive into website design or programming before they have begun the planning process on the business side. Let me re-state that. MOST begin designing the website before they have articulated what it is they intend to accomplish through the website. This is absolutely insane, given how much time, energy, money, and resources will be invested in the website.

Create a Masterpiece

By "masterpiece" I don't just mean visually beautiful. In my book, a website can only qualify as a masterpiece if it is capable of delivering results for your organization. Strategy is where the masterpiece begins.

Just as the artist envisions the sculpture within a slab of stone, it is your responsibility—and yours alone—to drive the strategy that will bring your website to life. Without deliberate, strategic direction, what is created may fail to support the needs, goals, and vision for your organization.

You are the composer. The team you assemble, whether internally or externally, becomes the orchestra performing the symphony. But it all starts with the music. You are the maestro, the strategist.

Save yourself

You can save yourself a great deal of time, money, and stress if you resist the temptation to rush and get something out there, and instead, drive the website process from a strategic point of view. Once you have developed your website strategy, you will be far better prepared to assess available technology, design, data, and solutions to determine which are most qualified to bring your strategy to life.

Real-World Insight

About two years ago, a client's decision to invest in a new website was derailed for more than a year because they did not have access to the information you now have in your hands.

The marketing director had enrolled in one of my SEO Training Programs. His number one goal was to improve the performance of the website in search, accompanied by goals to elevate brand, reach new markets, and streamline services to make more sense to visitors. Before we started working together, the owners of the company had defined their website budget of $2,500. He proceeded to interview a few website design firms and agencies and selected one willing to work within their budget, only to discover a few months into the process that the vendor was not capable of delivering what they needed. The outcome was disappointing to say the least. They selected their "second choice" firm and had a similar experience—precious time and money wasted.

After two false starts, defined largely by the perceived value of the website as a web brochure, the director of marketing knew he had to educate the executive management so that they could better appreciate the value of defining what they needed and allocating the resources needed to build a website that they could depend upon to support the goals of the organization. By the time they came around, his band-width was too full to cultivate what he learned and manage the website process on his own. He contacted me again to assist him further in developing a website plan for their company.

The director circled back to me and asked if I might be able to help them find a vendor that would deliver what they wanted. I recommended he create an RFP, define requirements (including a site map), and invite local web firms and agencies to submit proposals. I guided him through the process I have outlined for you in this book.

The RFP for the website redesign went out and they received a proposal from each company invited. The client was perplexed when the proposals varied so greatly after they had done so much work to define exactly what they needed and wanted.

It Only Takes One

As typically experienced when it comes to website proposals, it was next to impossible to establish an apples-to-apples comparison to facilitate the decision process. It was no surprise to me that each proposal they received was vastly different in specs, price, timeline, and focus. I have witnessed this firsthand since the 1990s when I worked at a new media firm and was responsible for defining proposal specs. Because there are no globally accepted definitions or requirements for website services, much is open to interpretation. This ends up being a recipe for disappointment (and sometimes disaster) for many consumers of web services.

Unfortunately, the client was not prepared for this. They were immobilized by the task of evaluating proposals because they were still faced with interpreting the many deviations from the specifications they had worked so hard to define. Because search was a major goal, the variations in how each proposal defined "SEO" (search engine optimization) was the first item to create frustration, followed by how many pages would be included (despite the inclusion of the web site map in the RFP), services included (design reviews, copywriting, forms, etc.) and what, if anything, would be required to maintain the website over time. Despite the request for WordPress, one proposal required use of their proprietary CMS (content management system), one would code it from scratch in HTML, and the third would use WordPress. At least someone was listening!

The result was that the client received only one qualified, accurately prepared proposal. In their mind, there was no choice but to go with this vendor. They engaged the firm and shortly after the project began, it became clear that the website was being pushed to fit into the confines of a theme the web firm had committed to and was not willing to deviate from.

Settling

Some items presented in the proposals took liberties with the non-defined aspects of the RFP which offered no value for this client, but rather served goals of the vendor. Remember, their primary goal is to make a profit from the services they provide. As a result, instead of moving toward a decision, the client was left to settle for what was proposed (even if they were not very clear on what they were getting) or to cease moving forward altogether. This was partly because of the criteria they chose to use when creating the list of potential vendors.

Over a year later, the project is under way, but not without a great deal of pain and anguish. The client is fully aware that with every month they have been delayed, they have also lost new business. Fortunately, this organization realized they needed help to better understand how to get the results they needed from the website investment. They sought my help and we began from the beginning by defining the strategy, requirements, and project specifications—the same process I present to you in this book. I am happy to report that the client is now in total control of their website and now know exactly what to expect from the completed website and how they will manage the asset moving forward. This is exactly where I want you to be—in control.

Been There, Done That?

It is very likely that if you have issued an RFP for a website, or simply contacted website companies for quotes, you have also received wildly varying proposals that made comparison impossible. The problem with RFPs does not lie in the inability of participating bidders to read and understand your request. The problem is web firms will present a solution to your request that best suits their organization's existing process and requirements for profitability.

It Doesn't Have to Be This Way

Needless to say, anyone would be confused when left to reconcile variances in project specs in order to make an informed decision. This challenge is compounded by the fact that most organizations that hire outside resources to build their websites do so every two, three, or five years, removing them from the dialogue and familiarity with terms that directly impact the ability of their investment to deliver results. Instead of moving forward and leading the web process, many organizations become so frustrated they either abandon the project, try to execute it internally, or pick a vendor and hope for the best. I hope to spare you from ever being subjected to such frustration.

The bottom line is despite the credibility of the firms responding to the RFP, moving forward with any one of their proposals would have failed to meet this client's objectives. They instinctively knew this but experienced difficulty in communicating exactly what they wanted and expected.

We will be walking through each aspect of the website to enable you to make informed decisions that will enable you to more deliberately articulate exactly what you want and get exactly what you ask for.

Best Recipes Start from Scratch

There is nothing like homemade pie or cookies, yet if you omit one key ingredient before baking, the results will yield a less-than-desirable outcome. (There's nothing worse than a flat cake or a cupcake with no flavor!) The same is true for websites. Each has its own unique flavor, yet there are key ingredients of a winning website that if omitted deplete the quality of the finished product. We will be exploring key ingredients for success, as well as the decisions that determine the "flavor" of the website, beginning with the website mission.

There are four paths to a website:

- Brand

- Research

- Comparison

- Purchase

Begin and End with Brand

Whether you are a household consumer brand or a local, family-owned establishment, your brand is one of the most valuable assets of your organization. When a visitor comes to your website by brand, it is typically in response to a direct referral by way of a human, search engine, or marketing effort.

Brand is more than a logo. Your brand is what others think or feel when they hear the name of your company, see your logo, read your brochure, watch your video, use your product, hear others talk about your product, and, of course, visit your website. The essence of a brand comes to mind instantly. For example, what do you think of when I mention *Trump*, *McDonald's*, or *Godiva*? A winning website reinforces the brand throughout the user experience—not just from a visual standpoint, but from a competitive perspective.

Because you cannot rely upon brand to reach new customers, you must proactively appeal to visitors by communicating brand values (whether it be quality, price, service, convenience, etc.) to win the hearts and minds of "ideal customers," one visit at a time.

What's Your USP?

The website strategy and mission come to life when you express your USP (unique selling proposition) through website design, SEO, content, and calls to action.

Even if most of your business comes from referrals, you can be sure that the first step a potential customer will take will be to conduct research on your brand. Don't believe me? What is the first thing you do when someone you know recommends a product, service, or brand? You conduct a search! Customers conduct some level of research, regardless of how they heard about your brand.

Think about your website. How might your website use brand to drive interaction, engagement, and conversion? Be sure to capture these thoughts as they come to you so that you have them when you are ready to explore this aspect of your website further as we progress through the planning process.

Chapter 9:

The Website Mission

The Website Mission is paramount.

Most organizations can tell you where they want their business to be in one year or five years, but few use these goals to guide the investment they will make to create the website responsible for supporting these goals online. When I work with an organization on any aspect of their website, e-business strategy, SEO, social media, or digital marketing, it is essential that I do so with a firm understanding of my client's objectives and goals. It is imperative you do the same.

The Anatomy of the Website Mission

Mission Possible

A good website mission statement explains, in one sentence, who you are, who you serve, what you offer, why you do it, where you customers are, when your offer is relevant, and how you do it (but not necessarily in that order).

For example, the mission for the website for this book (milliondollarwebsite.tv) is, "To empower others to own the website process, to make strategic decisions that leverage best practices to create a digital environment better prepared to compete online, to support goals, and to deliver ROI, regardless of budget."

Define the Mission

It is imperative that you define the Website Mission. You can measure performance only if you firmly understand what the website is expected to deliver.

Once you define the mission for the website, the strategic planning process can begin. Chances are your website has never had a mission before. Am I right? What about goals? Does your website have a charter to fulfill? Do you know how to measure success, and have you created the path for your customers to help you get there? Your website should be designed to serve the customer first, and your organization second. When your customers are happy, they will become loyal customers. Rather than muddying the waters, support internal goals with an intranet, password-protected content, or a separate environment altogether. The primary mission of the public website is to reach new customers, invite them to engage with your brand, and convert website visitors to loyal customers.

Once you have defined the website mission, everything else must be measured by this standard. If something doesn't support the mission, it is not vital to the project. Remember, the website is an investment, and the more focused you are, the greater the return will be.

Chapter 10:

Defining Website Strategy

Are you building a brand-new website, updating an existing one, or doing a total website redesign? The website strategy greatly enhances performance and reduces cost of ownership of the website over time.

Rob Garner, Vice President of Strategy at iCrossing, and author of *"Search and Social: The Definitive Guide to Real-Time Content Marketing"*, explains the importance of defining strategy before creating or re-designing a website:

"The most important thing you can do is to start out with a strategy. Before you start to build out, before you start to plan and really go to the next step that gets that project moving along, it is so important that you plan for certain things in the beginning, or else, at the end you might find yourself trying to re-do those things and it will cost you ten times more and you might only get one-tenth of the results that than you would if you had planned for them in the beginning."

The website strategy should be a high priority. As the document that you will use to define your goals and objectives, the website strategy will guide requirements, web design, architecture, SEO, content requirements, budget, scheduling, and ongoing management. Bottom line, a good strategy will save you time, money, and stress.

You have to know where you've been and where you are going before you can chart a path forward.

The Past

When redesigning or rebuilding a website, historical perspective can be invaluable.

As young as the Internet still is, it has a great deal of history. One of my favorite things to do when looking back in time is to use the "Way Back Machine" to see what a website used to look like. You can see what any website has looked like over time by entering the URL. A timeline will display various iterations of over 150 billion web pages archived beginning in 1996.

The Way Back Machine is collaborating with institutions, including the Library of Congress and the Smithsonian, to preserve a record of the Internet for generations to come. This is fun, and it can also be a little scary. For example, back in 2002 the first of 158 captures of the website for my digital marketing firm featured an animated .gif on the home page. (Yikes!)

Exercise:
Look at your website on the Way Back Machine, and look at it today. Is it worthy of preservation and archival as a representation of your brand?

Mining Data

One of the most logical places to interpret historical performance when planning a new website is to evaluate website analytic or statistical data. If you are planning a brand-new website, you want to begin with offline data. This can include direction from the business plan, collaboration between leaders within the organization, focus groups, sales, marketing, and customer service data from offline activity. If you are building a website for a brand-new organization, brand, or company, you will have to rely upon your business plan for guidance in planning forward.

Every website generates data that is most typically available through statistics, reporting, or tools like Google Analytics. Many organizations pass off monthly reporting with what is referred to as Google Analytics "Dashboard Report" or its equivalent in other programs. These 50,000 foot views provide a snapshot of performance for a specified time frame and can be managed to compare data sets to a previous season, month, or year. But there is much more gold in them there hills!

Useful web analytics enable you to customize dates, compare current data to the previous week, month, or year, and drill down into page-specific data that relates to SEO, usability, content, and conversion. Most marketing professionals and webmasters are not masters of the wealth of data available in Google Analytics, which is why I strongly suggest training. You can't make good decisions if you cannot interpret the data.

So, what should you be looking for? First and foremost, make sure your site is generating such data. And, if not, request that Google Analytics code or site statistics begin to be generated immediately. Some data is better than no data. Analytics provide valuable insight, even if only a month, two, or three are available; available data offers valuable insight you can use to make informed decisions about what programming languages are compatible with how your customers visit your website, what percentage access your site with a mobile device, and how many come to your website via search, referrals, or direct visits. Currently direct traffic reflects when website visitors key in your URL, visit via email, social media, or other source. Because how Google defines traffic does change, it is wise to check periodically to understand how traffic is being tracked.

Whether you or one of your team pulls the data together, some of the insights you want to glean from historical data include:

- Where do your **Visitors** come from? (Search, referral, email, social media?)

- What **Content** is viewed the most?

- Which of **Pages Viewed** received the most mobile visitors?

- Which **Landing Pages** deliver the most traffic from organic search?

- What are the most common **Entrance Pages** on your website?

- Which **Exit Pages** do visitors leave your website from?

- Which visitors mostly frequently completed **Conversion** to become customers?

- Which products were most frequently sought in **Site Search**?

- What **Traffic Sources** deliver the most visitors to your website?

   o **Search Engine Visits** via organic search engine results or paid ads

   o **Direct Visits** via URL entered into the web browser

   o **Referral Visit**s via a link from another website

- How effective are **Campaigns** in promoting conversion?

This barely scratches the surface of how you would evaluate a website. The data within each of these metrics are full of information qualifying marketing programs, effectiveness of SEO, reach of owned media, influence of social media, and so much more.

Let's take a look at real-world data to bring these concepts to life.

The Story of a Single Post

I posted a blog about a Southwest Airlines promotion that took down their website, paralyzed customer service, and upset many of the three million visitors they were targeting with a Facebook Flash sale. We explore the teaching moment created by this debacle further in chapter 25: "Be Prepared for Success." For now, we will focus on the post itself.

The post received 132 visits in a 48-hour span. Nice to know, but I need to know more if I want to gain a better understanding of how readers found the post, where they are located, and what they did once they got there.

Reviewing further, I see that visitors spent over six minutes on this particular post (outstanding by web standards). But where did they come from?

Of the total post readers, 65 percent arrived by way of RSS, meaning they clicked on a link generated by the RSS feed on my blog or where the feed was present. Because the blog RSS feed was included on my LinkedIn profile at the time, visitors could have arrived via the presentation of the post linking to the page.

The rest of the traffic came via Google organic search and social media platforms: Google+, LinkedIn, Twitter, and Facebook updates. I could see exactly which keyword phrases delivered visitors to the post, and I could see that 92 percent of those who arrived on this post were first-time visitors to my blog, 32 percent visited by way of a mobile device, and 90 percent were in the United States when they visited (which makes perfect sense because it was a post about a domestic American brand). The remaining 10 percent of visitors were from India, the United Kingdom, Canada, Israel, Switzerland, Spain, and France.

Feedback

As any experienced web professional will tell you, Google Analytics, or any form of website statistical data, are a vital part of managing the website. Analytics tell the story of your visitors and assist you in connecting the dots between goals and performance. When your goal is to reach and resonate with target audiences, it is imperative to know how effective your efforts are.

Analytics may tell you that visitors arrived via search, but they cannot tell you whether the page or post was effectively written and optimized unless you knew who your intended readers were and what the intended outcome would be. It is only when you measure the performance of actual visits against the intended outcome (defined by type and location of visitors, keywords used, and how well they aligned with the customer personas you created) that you will know how well assets were optimized.

Referencing your customer personas when evaluating analytics enables you to measure how effectively the website delivers what visitors seek and converts them to customers.

Embrace the Data

If you aren't sure how to extrapolate this data from your statistical reports or Google Analytics, you may find it worthwhile to take a Google Analytics class or webinar. We will periodically post various classes on the website: MillionDollarWebsite.TV

A comprehensive analysis of the existing website must be conducted. This analysis is designed to evaluate the website, measure and preserve the integrity of what has been effective, and identify opportunities to improve the environment to better support goals and objectives in the future.

Once you have completed the Website Worksheet (I provide a link at the end of the chapter), complete the Website Audit to determine how well your website has supported business goals to date.

The Present

How visitors currently respond to your digital environment is highly relevant. Up-to-date site analytics complemented by internal reporting will enable you to connect the dots between the website and conversion. Whether the goal is sales, demo requests, email opt-ins, whitepaper downloads, social media shares, event attendance, members, enrollment, offline visits, or any other number of outcomes, your current website offers timely insight that can be leveraged in the strategic planning process.

How your customers respond to your current website provides a snapshot of performance in the highly competitive digital landscape.

Do Not Flatter Your Competition

I can't tell you how often I've seen organizations approach building a website for their organization by referencing the website of a competitor, thinking that duplicating some or all of a competitor's website will enable them to replicate the success, search position, brand awareness, and market share of market leaders. The problem is the web doesn't work this way.

You must be able to clearly define your brand in the vast landscape of the Internet. If you intend to lure clicks away from your competitor, you must differentiate yourself clearly. When you emulate the competitor's brand visually, contextually, or through language, you increase the power of another brand. I'm confident that is not your intent, so let me show you how to glean insight from your competitors without helping them.

The following are straightforward guidelines based on the most frequently asked questions related to emulating the digital presence of your competition:

Creating a Truly Competitive Website

- Duplicating your competitors' metadata will not enable you to achieve their position in search engines.

- Copying content will not position you head-to-head with competitive websites. In fact, duplicate content can and will work against you amidst the latest search algorithm rules.

- Choosing a domain that closely resembles a competitor's domain only expands their perceived power in the marketplace. Choose a domain that reflects your brand and/or USP (unique selling proposition) that differentiates you from your competition.

- Copying design, branding, or the website user experience may entice customers not paying close attention, but that works both ways when visitors who thought they were visiting your website end up on a competitor's website. Tread carefully.

Behavioral Insight

Just as analytics tell the story of the past, current website analytics and/or statistics are invaluable when determining where you stand with competitors and customers at this moment in time. You should be able to map the path of visitors today, demonstrating where customers come from, where they go on the website, and what the outcome of their visit is. Comparing current data with that of previous years reveals which direction your website is trending.

Interpret Web Data Properly

One of the most common challenges with website analytics is how the data is interpreted. For example, just because your website receives visits via organic search doesn't mean the website is properly optimized. The mere reflection of user consumption of what you have presented on the web is most useful when you want to understand how useful your visitors found your website to be.

While gathering data that reflects how visitors consume the website, it is equally important you explore how to better serve your customers. This valuable insight is almost always available from those in your organization who interact with your customers. All you have to do is ask for it.

Tap Knowledge Within

Now is a good time to solicit feedback from every department impacted by your ideal customers. You will want to translate how these customers interact with your organization (from marketing to sales, customer service, HR, technical support, and everything in between) into how your website interacts with visitors. Requesting a behavior profile for each user will be helpful in advancing the user experience for all of the visitors to the new website.

The following are some tips on how to collect this information in the most meaningful way:

- Share the profile of your "ideal customer" with each department.

- Ask each department to outline their activity with these customers at every level of interaction as it relates to your "sales" cycle. The objective is to outline the steps that contribute to the transition from lead to prospect to closed customer (first contact, second interaction, before proposal, after proposal, before training, after training, etc.).

- Ask each department for a profile of website visitors that they **currently** interact with:

  o Demographics of those visitors (geography, age, gender, education, affiliations, etc.)

  o Common requests/problems

  o Common responses/solutions

  o Escalation policy (to whom do they refer visitors and why)

Generating the following reports using the following time frames provides key, up-to-the minute data:

Year to Year: Compare the past year to the year prior, or go as far back as you can.

Month to Month: Compare the past month to the month prior.

The following is a sample of the reports you can (and should) capture for each time frame:

- Unique Visitors

- New Visitors

- Search Engine Visits

- Unpaid Search Engine Visits

- Referrals

- Bounce Rate

- Pages Viewed (per visit)

- Time on Site (per visit)

- Total Mobile Visits

- Visits via Mobile Search

The data provided in these reports reflects which direction your website is moving. Because the landscape can change in the blink of an eye, it is imperative that your organization visit and assess this data regularly. You will be able to determine whether site performance is getting stronger or weaker, and identify specific events, trends, and behaviors that will impact the decisions you make to execute and fulfill your website strategy.

Be a Leader Not a Follower

The best use for competitor website(s) is as a benchmark to elevate your site to be better. I call this benchmarking. The objective is to make your website better than competitors' websites in at least one distinct way that is valuable to your target audiences. If this is not something you can achieve instantly or initially with your website, be sure to define a path to elevate your website above the competition over time and continually adapt it to the current "status quo."

One very desirable benefit to being innovative is media coverage. The media is hungry to cover fresh, new ideas, especially in trade and industry publications. This shouldn't be the driving force behind your strategy. However, if you really can think out of the box, your approach will attract the kind of media attention that could position you as a market leader.

Look into the Future

Plan your website for tomorrow, not today. The reality is that building a website takes time, and it's not something you will likely do more than once every year or two. Between the time you begin to plan your website to the time it goes live, rest assured the landscape in which you will compete (the Internet) will have changed.

Leverage e-business strategy, architecture, content organization, competitive differentiation, SEO, Internet marketing, social media, and all related digital activity from a marketing perspective.

By Chance - or by Design?

Can a website become a huge success without going through all the steps outlined in this book? I suppose it can. However, if your business depends on acquiring new clients or customers, why would you leave the success of such a vital part of your business open to chance? Websites that attract new visitors, clicks, conversion, media coverage, and the attention of their competitors are products of design, and I don't mean visual design. I mean on purpose—and it all begins with an e-business strategy.

Todd Keup, a former CIO, veteran web developer, programmer and owner of Magnifisites, who has been involved in the development websites since the early 1990's, illuminates the value of planning and communication in the design and development of a website;

"The biggest challenge we run into, bar none, has been trying to lead the client or the person we are working with, to organize their thoughts. The other end of the spectrum is the dream client who has already put together wireframes, identified color pallets, etc. We can then implement design and the technologies required to make sure that its secure, fast and that it is precise.

Who would we rather work with? We're obviously going to choose the latter. It's going to be a lot easier for us to deliver exactly what they intended. We are not going to struggle with communication because we don't have a game plan from the beginning. It's a much healthier, happier relationship...and much more gratifying for both parties.

My advice is to admit to yourself that you are going to have to do some of the homework, develop some of the content and put an outline together so that you get exactly what you want."

The e-business strategy is the foundational building block for your website, no matter how large or small it is. Defining your website strategy is imperative to facilitate the decisions that will drive everything from building the team that will build the website, determining what type of website to build, choosing vendors, building a budget, establishing a project timeline, beginning website design, writing content, performing SEO, and supporting advertising and marketing investments.

Defining Your Website Strategy

Before you initiate the website process it is imperative that you extract yourself from the thought that the website is a project. This is among the greatest flaws in how brands and businesses view their website.

The website is a fluid reflection of your brand within an ever-changing marketplace, the Internet. Just as your offer, service, brand, promotions, and price must continually adapt in order for your organization to maintain its competitive edge, your website must also evolve.

Your website is unlike any other business tool. Those who view the website as a static object, like a company brochure or earnings report, do so at their own peril. The website is a story that must continually adapt to the story teller and the audience. Your story may evolve only slightly over time. However, you can be sure that as your audiences become more savvy over time, they will expect and demand more from your website. Responding to your customers is vital if you wish to sustain your brand over time. It is imperative that you view the website as a living, breathing member of your team.

Over the years I have used a worksheet to assist in shifting a client's thinking from the website as an object to an extension of their business and goals. You can download the Website Worksheet at MillionDollarWebsite.TV for free.

I highly encourage you to complete the worksheet. It may seem like you are stating the obvious, and some of you may even think these topics have little to do with the website you need for your business. Please trust me. More often than not, when clients return the worksheet, they tell me how valuable it was for them to go through this process internally. It forced them to define business objectives that shape website strategy, search engine optimization, mobile, and digital marketing investments.

Chapter II:

Myths vs. Facts

It is amazing how much misinformation swirls around and how often myths influence how real businesses approach the Internet. So, let's address some of the most common myths.

Myth: Size Matters

Size does not matter, at least when it comes to the website budget. This may very well fly in the face of what you have been conditioned to believe. I do my best to explain how cost and quality do not always reconcile. How big the budget is does not ensure success when it comes to creating a winning website. The size of your website may be impacted by your budget (of time and resources). However, the abundance of solutions that leverage the latest developments in technology, software, and management go a long way to effectively and cost efficiently building a website.

Strategy is more important than the size of the budget when it comes to creating a quality website. Before you write a single word, begin the website design discussion, plan your timeline, or define the budget, you must first develop a solid strategy for the website. The website strategy will keep you on the straight and narrow. I walk you through the process of building a website strategy similar to the way I guide clients.

Time and knowledge will serve your mission far better than mere money. And, if all you have is money, my best advice to you is; spend it wisely.

Myth: You Must Speak Design and Code

You do not have to learn a new language to effectively communicate with the designers, programmers, and SEOs that will assist you in building a winning website.

When you are the driver of the discussion and can articulate your goals, the talented professionals that will breathe life into the website are better prepared to make suggestions and collaborate.

I would be remiss if I failed to illuminate the fact that many of those willing to offer their services in exchange for a fee are not entirely qualified to deliver a quality website. Believe it or not, seemingly successful businesses are often among the most unqualified. Don't be fooled by large client rosters and inflated quotes. Once you complete this book, you will be prepared to articulate very clearly what you need to be successful. It will be the web team or vendor's responsibility to translate how they will fulfill your requirements and achieve your goals. Do not allow smoke and mirrors to cloud the discussion. Request they respond to your business requirements item by item, and you will never have to revert to discussions in HTML, PHP, CSS or any other code.

Myth: Convert Customers Wherever They Are

The website should always be the primary destination. There are so many places to build your digital presence online these days that some have been lulled into believing they may not really need a full-blown website. Those who forgo the website do so at their own peril. Let me explain.

The web elite understand that integrating owned, earned, and paid media elevates the visibility and performance of the website, but the primary destination should always be the website.

Owned, Earned, and Paid Media

- Owned Media: Website pages, posts (RSS), press releases, promotions, news, product feeds, catalogs, email communications, whitepapers, polls, surveys, social media profiles, social media updates, posts, and comments, etc.

- Earned Media: Goodwill and favor provided by those outside the control of your brand, most typically through blog posts, reviews, comments, and recommendations on your digital properties and others across the Internet.

- Paid Media: Paid advertisements, banner ads, sponsored links, sponsorship, or underwriting of programs, etc.

Forrester Research created a well-structured graph illustrating the content that falls into each of these categories. I have provided a link to the chart on the website.

Leveraging each type of media extends the effective reach of your brand. The more connected you are to others on the Internet, the more "authority" you build with search engines. This is a little more complex than it sounds, so for the purpose of planning a *Million Dollar Website*, we focus on creating an environment ready and able to promote and receive these interactions. However, there is much more to be gained when this is executed strategically within your website marketing plan. (Perhaps that will be my next book.) But for now, let's focus on the relationship among owned, earned, and paid content to reach qualified audiences.

Owned, Earned, and Paid Media and the Website

Owned media is required if you wish to compete in today's marketplace. The website, the focus of this book, is the most powerful owned asset. Owned media includes blogs, video channels, social media profiles, posts, press releases, etc. Each of these directly impacts your brand and the effectiveness of the website.

The more *owned media* you offer, the more *earned media* you gain. When deployed strategically, the relationship between owned and earned media generates more authority for your website. As discussed in the chapter on SEO, authority is valuable to search engines, media, and customers. The Content chapter of the book addresses how to do this more specifically.

Paid media has its place in the mix; however, not every website requires paid programs. The web elite know that paid media delivers better results as part of a specific campaign, and it should never be relied upon as a primary or dominant source of website traffic.

Fact: The Source of Your Website Traffic Matters

The source of your website traffic most definitely does matter, especially in the wake of Google Penguin Updates.

Many people want to know the ideal balance of traffic sources, but this varies as every website and brand is unique. Owned, earned, and paid activity may fluctuate based on the selling season or any number of other compelling reasons that drive elevated activity.

Generally speaking, search should account for 50 percent of your website traffic, including paid and unpaid traffic. Referral and direct traffic account for the remainder of your traffic and are influenced by a variety of off-site actions such as email campaigns, social media activity, media coverage, a mention in a blog, promotion by affiliates, etc.

Myth: It Doesn't Matter Where Website Visitors Come From

Discussions about traffic sources are typically focused on links. The truth is relationships between links and websites known to be in "bad neighborhoods" can negatively impact search performance. The Google Penguin Update was designed specifically to identify unnatural link relationships.

My best advice is to keep it clean, promote link relationships with reputable websites, and closely monitor traffic sources to ensure you have a healthy balance between search engine, referred, and direct traffic sources.

Myth: Our Website Must Serve Our Organization

You must be in control of your digital footprint. However, the website on which you will depend to support your business must be dedicated to serve your customers. Resist the temptation to create a "wish list" that serves the egos and operational needs of the organization. Save that information for an Intranet, or a place out of sight from the public website.

The customer must be in control. Empowering visitors to find the information they seek and inviting them to interact with your brand is vital to the successful website.

Forget about what the website can do you for you. Put all of your focus on what you can do for them. Integrate operational, marketing, and revenue mechanisms into the customer experience whenever possible.

What a Difference a Little Bit of Strategy Can Make

The following is an example from a website project I led with million-dollar budget.

A retail home furnishings chain was investing significant dollars to build an online store to complement (not replace) the in-store sales of their brick-and-mortar stores and go head-to-head with the then-market leader, furniture.com. Building a home furnishings online store was a very innovative concept at this time (late 1990s) amidst speculation that people wouldn't be willing to purchase furniture they couldn't see or touch. We now know that consumers are willing to purchase just about anything online, especially when reviews and recommendations are present from those who purchased before them. The goal was to become the definitive online furniture store on the Internet in the markets where they had physical stores along the entire Eastern Seaboard, with potential to expand to nationwide sales.

One of the most advanced features of this web environment was the complete inventory of product. Every sofa, bed, table, chair, rug, and lamp was represented in the database, along with the exact specifications for each. Useful data, right? You wouldn't want to order a sofa that wouldn't fit in the room you were buying it for, would you? Each product page provided this information. This was powerful data on its own merit. But there was opportunity for much more.

Data is only useful if it can be applied in a meaningful way. As it turns out, I was fortunate enough to be working with some very creative designers at the time. We thought that data would come to life for the consumer if they could actually see the furniture of each room they were decorating over time. Form met function as we created the web's first interactive room planner. As the first website to deploy such an environment, the website created a new benchmark for the industry.

This interactive environment enabled customers to shop and pull items from the live inventory database into rooms created by the user. Customers could create an account, enter the dimensions of the room, add doors, windows, etc., and place furniture pieces anywhere in the room to see how they would fit, including rugs, tables, and lamps.

With a little "out of the box" strategy, I was able to introduce to the client a value-added experience that would differentiate them from the competition and promote conversion and loyalty with customers. Needless to say, the client loved the concept, even though it was a little ahead of its time. This powerful but easy-to-use tool created a quality user experience that added value to the consumer and encouraged them to stay and shop on the website longer and return to the website to retrieve "saved" rooms and product, promoting conversion in a way no retailer had ever done before.

If we had simply approached this website the way most retailers still do today, offering a catalog of product and a shopping cart, this site would never have fulfilled its potential. Instead, we put the needs of the customer first and were able to add value for both the customer and the company. The customer could put entire rooms together, virtually. The website enabled them to design rooms, purchase single pieces of furniture or entire rooms, and return to add furniture at any time, creating a long-term relationship with the retailer. Win-Win. Right?

Exercise:
Think about where the threshold is in your industry and what you can do to break through to provide a fresh, innovative approach to the problems your customers seek to solve.

Myth: The Website Should Look like All Other Websites in the Industry

Being different requires courage. And, fortunately, when planned well, such courage is typically rewarded. Your website must do something better than the competitors' websites. If you cannot identify something truly unique about your brand, create a new way to solve a problem.

How you deliver your message is as important as having one. As I demonstrated with the previous *Million Dollar Website*, enabling your visitors to interact with your brand is what brings key differentiators to life and can make all the difference your website's effectiveness.

Still stumped? The following are some suggestions to get your wheels turning:

- If your best clients are informed, set out to be the leading source of information. Create an online magazine within your website, create a video TV show to discuss the greatest challenges that your product or service solves, field customer service questions on an Internet radio show, and/or publish a blog highlighting industry news that reinforces your USP, new products, or tips. If your ideal clients require speed and efficiency, make access to content and conversion quick and easy. Create a mini menu that features links to key content and calls to action.

- If your clients or customers demand high levels of quality and service, elevate the value of your offering in content, but also offer live chat and click-to-call as a "concierge" service to do the work for clients. I recommended this for a luxury travel company and it worked beautifully for them as it differentiated them from competitors and elevated their desire to provide personal service because they knew their conversion rate was near 100 percent when they got clients on the phone.

- If your customers are price sensitive, define a competitive pricing strategy, create a form for customers to report lower prices they may find elsewhere to get a special offer or matching price, and use that to differentiate yourself. If you will always beat a competitor's price, state it.

Perhaps you don't always have the lowest price, but you sell product made only in the United States. You would want to promote the benefits of product made in the United States, or identify issues created by products manufactured in other countries by featuring recalls of foreign product as a way to elevate appreciation for American-made product.

- If you have received top industry awards or consistently rate #1 in your market based on consumer reviews and testimonials, share it—proudly.

Creative problem-solving could greatly enhance your ability to serve customers in any of the Three Phases of the Purchase Decision.

Myth: Open Source, Template and CMS Websites Are Fine As-Is

It is imperative that you understand that as powerful as Open Source platforms like WordPress, Drupal, Joomla, and others are, they, and the widgets and apps that are used to enhance them, are only as good as the strategy that drives them.

Bill Grunau, Chief Strategy Officer, Co-President of Esotech, Inc., Author of *"Own Your Future"* and a kindred spirit in all things digital, has a Company Blog Post (link from the website) that shares some of the same cautions I present to those choosing a platform for their website that preserves ownership and promotes performance.

The last thing you want to do is to buy a website package of 5 to 10 pages without creating a compelling opportunity for visitors to interact with your brand based on your core value proposition. Even though you've not read the entire book, I hope you already recognize that building a website requires an approach unique to the organization it represents. Your website must be unique to your brand and reflect a path unique to the relationship you have, or will have, with your customers.

Fact: The Customer Is in Charge

The website must empower customers to control their experience in whatever way that is relevant to their goal at the moment they visit, whether it is the first, fourth, or fortieth time they visit the website.

Website visitors validate the value of what the website offers with their actions. Clicks, views, reviews, votes, requests, purchases, comments, "Likes," +1's, shares, and recommendations to others are the ultimate reward for providing your target audience with what they want, the way they want it. Knowing what, exactly, your audiences want is not something to be assumed. (You know what they say about assuming.) If you watch, listen, analyze, and test, you are sure to get it right—or very close to right—the first time. If you make assumptions, you will be greatly disappointed by the results, wondering why your audiences have not responded to what you were sure would delight them. We will explore how to use the data generated by your audiences to make informed decisions about what to offer on your website. For now, suffice it to say that the primary goal is to offer what your audiences seek and you will be rewarded time and time again.

On 24/7

When you invest in a website, chances are you do not enter into an agreement with the vendor thinking that you were going to invest many months of time and your hard earned capital to create an entity incapable of bringing a single new customer to your business on its own merit. Yet, when you hand over your digital destiny to an outsider, there is a chance that this is exactly what you will get. If you've hired someone to build a website for you in the past, did you get what you hoped you would get? Sure, you may have been a little naïve and trusting in the past.

Your website is your 24/7 receptionist, sales representative, customer service department, consumer education center, and it can be even more, depending on what type of organization you have. As such, it is vital that the website become an extension of your business, brand, and relationships. Your goals will drive the decisions on what content and mechanisms make the most sense, but this could mean anything from a simple email opt-in, contact form, knowledge base, e-commerce, forum, live chat, or any number of features that will transform your website into a lead generator, customer relations provider, and business asset.

Vital to Every Business

Website strategy is most likely the very first contact point you will have with a majority of your customers, whether they find you on their own, are directed to the site from your advertising or marketing efforts, or are referred by a strategic partner, media coverage, referral, or satisfied customer. It is imperative that your website look, feel, and engage with each visitor the way you would great them in person. In other words, the website must be consistent with your brand experience. If you are known for your excellent service in brick-and-mortar locations, your customers will expect the same online. The same applies if you have the lowest prices in town, are the most secure, have the best selection, best quality—you get the idea.

Your website is the digital extension of your business, 24 hours a day, 7 days a week, 365 days a year. The website strategy should reflect and support your organization's mission statement. In fact, the mission is a very good place to start when developing a *Million Dollar Website* strategy.

Chapter 12:

3 Phases of the Purchase Decision

Regardless of the industry, customers go through a three-stage decision-making process before they make a purchase decision. This can happen over seconds, minutes, hours, or months. Understanding these behaviors is vital to the success of a website.

It is imperative that your website engage your customers according to whatever level they are in when they visit your website for the first time, second time, or fiftieth time. Because we will rely upon these three phases in Architecture, Planning, SEO, Design, and Content, I want to introduce you to each of the three phases of the purchase decision now.

3 Phases of the Purchase Decision

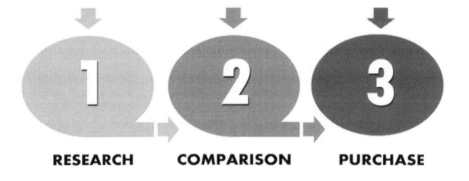

RESEARCH   COMPARISON   PURCHASE

Everyone talks about conversion. Few dig deeply enough to understand that the conversion of visitors will vary based on what phase of the purchase decision they are active in: Research, Comparison, or Purchase.

Placing 100 percent of the website's focus on closing the deal before making your case is like walking up to someone and asking them to marry you without first making an introduction and getting to know one another. Just as some arranged marriages can work, so can conversion-only websites, but why would you leave the other two-thirds of potential customers who are in research and comparison mode to competitors?

I have effectively leveraged these phases in website strategy, planning, SEO, design, content, and conversion of websites of all sizes in multiple industries. I will show you how meet your customers where they are to improve visibility, clicks, and conversion. Your website will be prepared to deliver what each visitor needs to make the decision to buy. I wrote a post on how optimization for all three phases of the purchase decision impacts conversion for Search Engine Watch, which you can access via the website: MillionDollarWebsite.TV

The 3 phases of the Purchase Decision offer unique opportunities to reach new customers, promote key differentiators, invite conversion, promote brand awareness, and grow market share. Remember to connect the dots between the 3 phases and each of your customer personas to ensure success.

The 3 Phases are vital to:

- Website Strategy

- SEO

- Architecture and Content Organization

- Content

- Conversion

- Promotion

- Ongoing Management

Research Phase

When customers begin seeking a solution to a problem, they conduct research. Research does not begin with brand. Think about it. When you begin shopping for a car, vacuum, computer, or software, you likely begin searching for a product that meets your specific criteria. Your website must specifically address the criteria used by your customers to find a solution to their problem. Because customers often do not know exactly what they need until after they have conducted research, it is your responsibility to ensure your website delivers that information. This approach is especially effective in the context of search.

Research Begins with Search

Most consumers conduct research online, beginning with search, which is why research is such a vital part of website SEO.

Globally, 89 percent of consumers use search engines for purchase decisions. The percentage of customers who turn to search when making a purchase decision is even higher for the United States (90 percent), the United Kingdom (90 percent), Canada (93 percent) and France (96 percent) (Fleishman Hillard, 2012).

Search should be a vital source of traffic for every website. I address specifics of the 3 Phases as they relate to search in the SEO chapter.

Conversion Opportunity

Some customers will learn enough from your website to make a decision or advance to the Comparison or Purchase phase of the decision.

Conversions for those in research mode can be as simple as entering an email address to receive access to a whitepaper, a consumer guide, "tips for buying," a reference tool, a free sample, a demo, or a free initial consultation. We'll discuss more options in the content goals section, but the bottom line is you want to be relevant when the website visitor is in the initial phases of making a decision if you wish to be a contender. The more information you offer to the customer in the Research phase, the more clicks to content on your website, which deepens your relationship with the potential customer and enhances your authority.

Exercise: Identify what you will offer and how you will measure a conversion for each of your customers in Research mode.

Research naturally leads the customer to comparison. Only after customers conduct this initial research to know what, exactly, they are looking for can they begin to identify contenders eligible for purchase.

The Comparison Phase

Your customers enter the Comparison Phase when they have enough information to begin examining which product, service, or solution best meets their needs. They have likely narrowed it down to two or three solutions. This is your chance to win the heart and mind of each individual customer by differentiating your solution from your competitors. I cannot stress this enough. If you do not explain what makes your solution better than the others, who will?

We touch upon this further in the chapters on SEO, Design, and Content. For now, we will focus on Comparison as the opportunity for your brand to become a trusted resource for the customer.

Content is key in differentiating your brand from your competition. To take advantage of those in this phase, you must consider the many ways that customers will research the solution that you wish to provide and then convey why you are the better choice.

A Quick Word about "The Competition"

Competitors are not limited to those you believe to be your competition. Your competition is every brand customers may *perceive* to be your competition, as well as those you compete against online.

When customers conduct research online, your competitors are every brand that appears above or below you in search engine results, mentioned in blogs, covered by industry publications, sponsors of events, reviewed on other websites, listed in directories, etc.

I realize accepting the scope of the landscape in which your brand competes can be daunting. Yet, it is imperative you understand who your customers are comparing you to if you wish to convert that visitor to a customer.

Leave Nothing to Interpretation

Unlike a face-to-face meeting or a live interaction with a customer, it is imperative that your website spell out clearly exactly what makes your brand worthy of the sale. Use text, visuals, video, and customer interaction to differentiate your solution, one person at a time.

Comparison charts, demo videos, special reports, reviews, testimonials, and display maps should be used to illustrate your USP (unique selling proposition). Include industry recognition, accreditation, awards, and security and/or privacy icons that add credibility or promote trust and authority.

Let me share an example to illustrate why this matters.

Mom-and-Pop Shop Had "Secrets"

A family-owned retail chain that specializes in uniforms and tactical gear for police, fire, special forces, government agencies, etc. came to my digital marketing firm for SEO. This business was started decades earlier by the owner's parents. It was literally a mom-and-pop shop that was growing quickly, and the owners were intent on increasing market share in the national marketplace.

What you would never know by visiting their old website was that they had served over a million customers, many of whom are agencies and departments that they have served for many years. This is no small feat. In addition, they actively patrolled (no pun intended) the Internet to make sure they had the lowest prices on key items that were purchased often.

Applying the 3 Phases

To improve visibility in search to those in the Research phase, we optimized product listings and their low prices, which attracted clicks. To differentiate this family-owned business from its competitors in the Comparison phase, we emphasized the qualities of this business that would promote trust with their "ideal customers": police, fire, and Special Forces departments. We included a hit list of enhancements:

- Company was family owned (which resonates with the values of their ideal customers).

- Company had served over a million customers (promoting trust by association, demonstrating service to the peers of website visitors).

- Age of the business—this business was founded over 40 years ago (which promotes perception of a legitimate business online).

- Company was committed to selling a select group of staple products at the lowest price on the Internet with a price-match guarantee.

In summary, we were able to optimize their website to compete in search for research, comparison, and conversion. As a result, the website achieved top #1, #2, and/or #3 positions on Google (and other search engines) for keyword phrases for customers who were seeking brand name merchandise at discount prices from a company that delivered personal service to agencies, municipalities, groups, and government contracts, in addition to individuals.

Oops.

The online store delivered and the company enjoyed a competitive position and sales. That is, until they decided to replace the optimized website with another shopping-cart website without maintaining improvements. Unfortunately, they did this on their own months later. This "improvement" inadvertently omitted every bit of SEO and optimization to promote conversion. The website has since disappeared from search results for anything other than brand.

Danger, Danger Will Robinson!

I shared this story with you so that you will understand how what you do not understand can, and often will, cost you big. All the time, money, and energy invested in optimizing their website was essentially lost.

Please, please, please consult your team, or hire a consultant for a few hours before making big website changes. This is where a little bit of planning could have preserved this business' competitive advantage, sustained revenue, and continued return on the investment made.

An update on this business:

After visiting one of the brick and mortar stores, my husband shared that he met one of the owners. After he introduced himself, they lamented how their business had enjoyed better results with the website we had optimized for them and that they definitely could use help in regaining lost ground. Their bottom line took a direct hit from a decision they made without consulting those who helped them achieve the success they had enjoyed. Hopefully you will learn from their mistake.

And, I hope your wheels are turning. How will you present your story so that it is compelling and differentiates you from the competition?

This is where the work in the planning of the website becomes more tangible. If you are unable to define how best to differentiate your brand to compete and win in the Comparison phase of the purchase decision, you will need to work through the competitive portion of the Website Strategy chapter. Hone in on what, exactly, will help you tell your story and win new customers 24 hours a day, 7 days a week, 365 days a year.

Calls to Action for Those in Comparison Phase

Aside from the obvious (asking for the sale), you can promote conversion that will keep you front of mind as they continue making their decision.

Invite visitors to opt-in with their email address for special offers, discounts, loyalty programs, etc. You could offer information that will help them make a more informed decision, such as a "buyer's guide," a head-to-head comparison chart that includes known competitors, and/or sharing reviews of third-parties such as industry publications and media. Offer the assistance of an expert, a free initial consultation, or a free quotation. When you have more locations than your competitors, say so. Include a location-search feature and track the use of this feature. If you differentiate yourself on price, offer to beat competitors' pricing, and offer a way for them to request a quote, or share a competitor's price and track it as a Comparison conversion. When you offer features that competitors do not offer, invite customers to request (by submitting an email) a demo, webinar, or free training class that highlights these features and track as a conversion. Do whatever makes it easier for your customers to differentiate you from competitors and make a decision.

Exercise:

Identify how you will differentiate yourself and how you will track the conversion of each customer in the Comparison phase.

Empower visitors to make an informed decision and you are well on your way to the Purchase.

Purchase Phase

Converting visitors to customers directly impacts the bottom line. The easier you make it for a visitor to find what they are looking for (especially when they have returned from Research and Comparison visits), the easier it will be to close the deal.

Surprisingly, many websites do a great job in telling their story online but forget to ask for the sale. You would be amazed by how many more conversions a website can generate by simply asking. I've seen it over and again, without fail.

Always Ask for the Sale!

"Purchase" could mean any number of things, depending on your website's mission. For some it will be an e-commerce transaction. For others, it could be a request for a proposal, a registration for an event, membership enrollment, submission of an application, media inquiry, investor capital, opt-in to an email, or any number of conversion-centric actions.

Most conversions will be facilitated in one of three ways: through a shopping cart purchase, submission of information through a form of some type, or sharing with others. Conversions are easy to track in Google Analytics when you create a unique completion, thank-you page, or destination page designated for each conversion type and identify them in Google Analytics.

Words to the wise regarding Purchase conversions:

- Be consistent

- NO SURPRISES

- Make conversion the easiest thing to do on the website.

Visitors ready to purchase do not like surprises. The website must provide the intuitive, interactive environment visitors have come to expect. You may have only one chance to win a customer, so be sure to remove all barriers.

Bees to Honey

Sometimes it helps to sweeten the deal. Don't be afraid to offer an incentive to inspire action. Offering an expiration date on promotions will create a sense of urgency. Align offers to external events, like an industry conference, holiday, special event, etc. All offers and special promotions should support the integrated marketing plan and business goals.

Prevent Abandonment

There is nothing more disheartening than to have visitors add items to their shopping cart but never complete the sale. Shopping carts for many online transactions result in a very high abandon rate. Typically this is the customer responding to new information not previously revealed during the Research and Comparison phases of the decision-making process. If the customer would have weighed this information into their decision, the introduction of new information at this late stage is often perceived to be sneaky or covert, so they decide to take their business elsewhere.

Exercise: Identify the mechanisms you will offer to convert each of your personas.

Got the Sale? GOOD!

You must be proactive in nurturing the new relationship you have just earned.

Good news spreads like wildfire. In today's digital landscape, word-of-mouth marketing (WOMM) is more powerful than ever. Once you have won a new customer, chances are they have the ability to influence others who could also become customers. I address the dynamics of how to leverage the network of your customers in my next book *Spheres of Influence*. For now, let's focus on inviting your customers to be a part of your brand experience.

Web 2.0

Inviting customer interaction on the website can be achieved in a variety of ways, from customer reviews on specific products, Facebook "Like" or Google+ buttons, testimonials, audio or video interviews, or a referral or recommendation. Data has shown that online customers trust reviews of strangers, as well as their trusted network over advertising. Websites like Amazon.com, TripAdvisor.com, Angie's List, and Yelp.com have built their businesses by including consumer reviews. So, it stands to reason that inclusion of feedback from real-world customers will resonate with new customers.

Whether you call it social media, web 2.0, or anything else, the objective remains the same—to build a level of confidence and trust with new customers that have not yet encountered your brand. Obtaining reviews for consumer businesses is often easier than it is for business to business (B2B) companies and consultants. However, video testimonials and written testimonials of clients that emulate the "Ideal Customer" will go a long way in attracting more of the same.

Be Your Customer

Exercise:

One of the easiest, low-tech ways to "reality check" how well the website will appeal to each of your customers is to put yourself in the place of each persona created to represent your ideal customers. Are others like you visible on the website? What can you do to help ideal customers identify with your brand?

Chapter 13:

SEO

The Eyes Have It

If you built the best hotel in the world on the top of a mountain that was inaccessible by land, sea, or air, your chances for success would be greatly diminished. If you build a website that your customers cannot find, your chances for success are no better. To the web elite, the Holy Grail in the world of websites is to reach new audiences, entice qualified visitors to your website, and convert those visitors into loyal customers.

The most powerful, cost-effective method to achieving visibility over time is to appear at the top of organic, or natural, search results achieved through search engine optimization (SEO).

I admit, because of the complexity of search engine algorithms and the frequency of changes that can impact a website's performance, SEO can be intimidating. I assure you that SEO is not smoke-and-mirrors, trickery, or, as some would have you believe, "dead."

The truth is, a very large percentage of professionally designed websites do not perform in search. In fact, you may be astounded to know how often web vendors release websites that fall pitifully short of meeting even the basic needs of the brand, forcing clients to go back into planning mode for a redesign almost as soon as they are completed.

SEO is complex because the search engine algorithms are continually changing and intentionally designed to prevent you from "beating the system." In Fall of 2011 at a conference I was speaking at, Matt Cutts from Google explained that Google's algorithm consists of around 200 variables, some of which are influenced by as many as 50 signals which are constantly changing, in addition to major updates such as Panda, Freshness Update, Google Plus Your World, and any number of other changes to the search engine environment. As a result, NO ONE can promise you page 1 position on Google, EVER.

Google explicitly warns against firms that assert such promises:

"No one can guarantee a #1 ranking on Google.

Beware of SEOs that claim to guarantee rankings, allege a "special relationship" with Google, or advertise a "priority submit" to Google. There is no priority submit for Google. In fact, the only way to submit a site to Google directly is through our Add URL page or by submitting a Sitemap and you can do this yourself at no cost whatsoever."

I have provided a link to this statement on the website.

One thing I will add is that despite the invitation to submit your website, Google maintains its right to include the website in the index, or not.

Anyone who has tried their hand at SEO, paid for SEO services, or hired a search engine optimization expert to achieve top position in search, understands that achieving top rank is far easier said than done.

I live and breathe website optimization and SEO every day. I could write an entire book series on search engine optimization. We won't have time or space to dive into detailed SEO methods in this book. However, because SEO is such a vital part of a successful website, I do provide vital information to ensure the website you build will be better prepared to fulfill its potential in supporting your goals. After all, what good is a fabulous website if no one can find it?

SEO Reality Check

SEO has become much like the website industry. Many talk about it, many say they do it, yet few do it well. Most brands assume that the website will be optimized for search. In fact many highly reputable firms talk about SEO when quoting the project but omit it from the contract and present it as an add-on after the website is complete. Far too many businesses are only told after investing in the creation of the website, that SEO was not included and must be added after the fact.

For the web elite, SEO is as vital to a website as the domain and a landing page. Without optimization, a website will not meet its full potential in search.

Simon Heseltine, director at AOL Inc. / Huffington Post Media Group (HPMG), who heads up search engine optimization (SEO) for all AOL properties, is a contributor to Search Engine Watch, and teaches SEO at Georgetown University, says it best:

"If the search engines can't crawl your site, they can't find your content, and therefore neither will your potential customers when they're searching for your goods / services. If your pages aren't optimized to mention what your products / services are, then they're not going to be found.

The search engines can only work with the data you give them, and they can only extrapolate so much from that data. You need to help them to help you, and that's where SEO comes into play.

Now if your site competes with one of the sites I work on, please feel free to ignore what I've said and make my job easier, otherwise help yourself by helping the search engines through optimizing your content."

SEO is one of the most powerful tools a website can deploy to compete for and win customers. SEO is not an add-on. It is not an afterthought. The web elite understand that effective SEO is part of the website planning process and requires a very methodical and deliberate approach if it is to effectively enable a website to perform in the ever-changing search environment.

Before getting into specifics around SEO, it is imperative to understand the search engine landscape. Many who actively "do" SEO often overlook the current landscape, or are unaware of best practices that have evolved from the beginnings of the competitive search landscape. Those of us who have been getting our hands dirty with SEO over the past 10 to 13 years share a deeper perspective that I share with you in this chapter.

A Historical Perspective Pays

Search has changed quite a bit over the past decade, and the pace of evolution has increased exponentially. Search engines use algorithms to calculate what appears at the top of search engine results. These algorithms change significantly and often. Believe it or not, search engines are not out to trip-up those who wish to reach customers in search. Instead, their primary goal is to deliver the best possible result to those conducting the search. Google is intensely dedicated to preventing those attempting to spam or trick search engines from gaming the system. As a result, over the past year, Google Penguin and Google Panda updates have sent many SEO firms packing. The methods they used to create revenue streams either no longer work or are no longer profitable, so many have turned to paid search and social media to replace former SEO service revenue streams. Keep this in mind if you suddenly find yourself being bombarded with offers to invest in paid programs or to abandon SEO and replace it with social media. Incorporating social media into your overall SEO strategy can be quite beneficial, but paid search is a totally different animal that will not improve your organic search performance.

The Players in Search

You will often hear about Google in the context of search. There is a reason for this. In the United States, Google has remained a dominant player in search on both desktop and mobile devices for a very long time. They were not the first search engine, but they have arguably become the gold standard in search since they entered the space in 1998.

Serving Billions

Every month comScore publishes search engine share for the previous month. For years now, Google has far exceeded Yahoo, Bing (Microsoft), AOL, and others in facilitating the largest number of searches. For the month of August 2012, comScore reported search engine share for the 17 billion core searches conducted in that month.

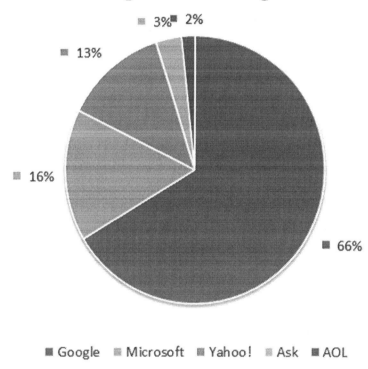

Search Engine Share: August 2012

■ Google   ■ Microsoft   ■ Yahoo!   ■ Ask   ■ AOL

- 66% (11.3 billion) on Google Sites

- 15.9% (2.7 billion) on Bing Sites (owned by Microsoft)

- (2.2 billion) on Yahoo! Sites

- 3.2% (550 million) on the Ask Network

- 1.7% (292 million) on AOL

Google gets a great deal of attention from SEOs because Google is responsible for the lion's share of searches, and because it is often the most difficult search engine on which to achieve results. A successfully optimized website can achieve top rank in Google, as well on Yahoo, Bing, and other search engines.

SEO Is Much More than Keywords

Far too many brands put all their energy into keywords. The use of keywords to qualify a website in search has been useful to frame content and optimize websites. However, websites cannot compete on keywords alone. Putting all your eggs into the keyword basket will not be enough. Not now, and most definitely not in the future.

Google's "Intel Inside" Is Not Search

In October 2007, Google's VP of Search Products and User Experience Marissa Mayer, (Now CEO of Yahoo!), announced that Google's "Intel inside" was not search but data. Not many in the search or marketing industry paid attention to this then or now. They continue to view Google as just a search engine.

What we now know, with the advent of Google Shopping, Google Maps, Google Voice, Google Docs, Google Glass, Google's Self-Driving Car, and Google Now is that aggregation of data acquired through Google services enables the development of the artificial intelligence that will forever change how we live, work, and play.

All search engines seek data. Simon Heseltine emphasizes this:

"Search engines can only work with the data you give them, and they can only extrapolate so much from that data."

The search engines can work only with what data the website provides them, making it imperative that you be as deliberate as possible in generating that data.

Word Index to Knowledge Graph

In February 2012 Google announced that it would be moving from the word-based index to the Knowledge Graph. In May 2012, it was officially launched. In a blog post, SVP of Engineering Amit Singhal said, *"This is a critical first step towards building the next generation of search, which taps into the collective intelligence of the web and understands the world a bit more like people do."*

You can learn more by viewing the post and video prepared by Google. (Singhal, 2012) A link to this post is also provided on the website.

Months later, this shift has eluded most in the SEO industry because they built their methods and revenue streams on keywords. The business model of SEOs should not drive your approach to website optimization. It is incumbent upon you to embrace Google's desire to gather information about your brand. Google is seeking connections among people, places, and things. That is exactly what you must be prepared to deliver.

In the Knowledge Graph, Google is seeking the most relevant information about your brand; the people in the organization; those influenced by your products, services, and interaction; and how they share their opinion with others.

Below you can see how the Google Knowledge Graph collects information from around the web (presumably through search index) for brands and people.

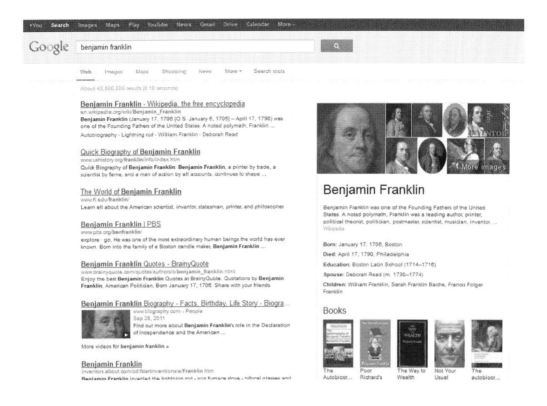

The Knowledge Graph appears as enhanced search engine results. Google's source is the data presented by websites across the web. The volume and speed of data being created is nothing short of mind-numbing.

Big Data

Every day 2.5 quintillion bytes of data are created.

Big Data is a relatively new concept that defines data generated by purchase transactions, call records, digital images, videos, posts to social media sites, and much more. This sea of data is generated by digital interaction and can provide insight into customer behavior. It also creates the competitive landscape in which your website and brand will compete. This is why optimizing a website for keywords will not be enough as the web matures. Search engines are looking beyond metadata to aggregate data to drive search. Because the words you place in metadata may not match a search as well as the content on the page, search engines have begun to include on-page data (content) in their calculations for search position.

Here's how Google explains it: "Google's generation of page titles and descriptions (or "snippets") is completely automated and takes into account both the content of a page as well as references to it that appear on the web" Reference: Google Webmaster Tools.

Knowledge Graph

Google has become much more than search. They are a data aggregator, content publisher, and are actively developing artificial intelligence to power driverless cars and glasses that serve as mobile screens. In September 2012 California Governor Jerry Brown pulled up to Google headquarters in Mountain View, California, to sign legislation that would enable Californians the ability to do the same. The robot-driven cars are expected to populate California freeways and beyond.

Kind of sounds like the movie *Matrix,* doesn't it? So what does this have to do with search?

Artificial Intelligence Requires Data—Your Data

Google could never have developed the artificial intelligence for the "brain" of these driverless cars without the unimaginable volume of data that they have collected through search, email (Gmail), voice (Google Voice), Chat, Google Checkout, Maps, Profiles, Places, News, Images, Website Analytics, Webmaster Tools, and a multitude of other applications. This knowledge is the brain behind the instant, predictive display of search results that refresh with every letter you type. These results become personalized by user when they are logged into any Google account. These factors have made it much more difficult for brands to determine exactly how well the website is performing in search. We explore how to operate in this search environment throughout this chapter. The high-level goal is to deliver a quality website with useful content with authority.

Relevance

Because data is valuable, content is king—not just any content, but content that is valuable and actionable by your target audiences. When your website consistently delivers the most qualified, relevant content related to the problem Internet users are seeking to solve, your website is more likely to perform better in search. The chapter on Content expands on best practices for creating good content.

The more relevant your content is, the more qualified your website is to appear in search engine results.

Over the years I have found that creating quality landing pages are vital to achieving top search engine rank. Relevance applies to performance of paid search campaigns very much the same way. Landing pages are extremely valuable and worthy of the time and energy required to be effective.

Because each of your customer types will search for content differently, I cannot stress enough the importance of developing the personas covered in chapter 6, "Who Do You Love", to guide your SEO efforts.

Authority

Authority also factors into the search algorithm. Authority can be defined as how accurate, useful, and relevant the content delivered by a specific source is over time— not just on your own website, but across the Internet. The relationships among your website and social media profiles, updates, mentions in the media, blog posts, reviews, etc. are important ingredients to building authority in the eyes of search engines.

Own It

Ideally, your website should be the primary and most authoritative source of data about your brand on the web. The more interaction you attract with, about, and around your brand and website, the greater your influence online. This includes history, brand messaging, products, services, reviews, people, stock information, career opportunities, events, news, and information. Authority is another factor search engine algorithms calculate when determining which results are most qualified to display at the top of results.

Authorship

Authorship has become a hot topic in the context of Google's recent search changes designed to connect people with what they say and where they say it. This can be highly beneficial when managed properly. Once you have established a credible reputation, your authorship becomes more valuable and desirable to others, so it must be protected. Evaluate the quality of the website and how posts are published and distributed before guest posting on another website.

It is important that the humans posting RSS content (blog posts) be identified as authors. This also applies when guest posting on another website or blog. This gives the author proper credit, often linking them to their own company website or blog, and enables search engines to identify the individual and any authority they may carry. This is why established authors are highly desirable as guest authors on websites owned by others, and why authors benefit from writing for other entities.

Guest Blogging

Google has come out to say that quality blog posts are a good thing. In fact, in a recent video, Matt Cutts explained Google's position on authors and links. He did establish that in the eyes of Google, quality authors, like Danny Sullivan of Search Engine Land or Lisa Barone of Overit, are credible, and as such, may be invited to guest post on other websites. This is how my relationship as a writer for Search Engine Watch works as well. Guest bloggers can be an asset when they are credible and post original content to your website.

Do Not Copy

Cutts does specifically caution about the re-purposing and tweaking of posts, or what some call "spinning," for distribution on multiple domains. Remember, Google is extremely effective in identifying any form of duplicate content. Cutts also cautions about over-zealous linking. This applies to website pages as well as posts. In these scenarios, Google may perceive the quality of content, links, and author as "spammy," reducing the quality of the posts, and it may penalize one, or all, of the affiliated websites and domains in search rank. Visit the website for the link if you'd like to view Matt's entire video post.

Google Is Not Out to Get You

You expect quality results when you search, so it makes sense that your audience would expect the same. Google has built an empire around delivering the best information. So, it makes sense that the more accurate, broad, and deep the data is on your website, the better the site will meet the needs of those who search.

Search results are no longer displayed as static SRPs (search engine result pages). Today, real-time search populates results with every keystroke in a search bar. Predictive results are based on past searches and what others have found to be quality results. Proven methods from the early days of SEO have sustained the evolution of such changes, making it possible for brands to compete in this environment. Algorithm and display changes can be frustrating to those new to SEO and can definitely keep even the most seasoned SEOs on their toes.

Different Strokes

A keyword search on Google, Yahoo, Bing or AOL produces different results. The same search on Google in three different locations will produce different results for each location. Each search engine has its own "rules" for search which actively parse through the data online using its own algorithms to display what it believes to be the best results for a specific search query.

Behind Each Search is a Human with a Question

If you keep this in the back of your mind throughout every phase of the website planning, design, content, and SEO process, you will fare better than most. Search is a direct connection between the person conducting the search and the most recent, relevant content on the web—in real time.

The introduction of instant, real-time, and predictive search may have significantly decreased the amount of time it takes for someone to type in a keyword, or even part of a word, before viewing results. However, if you are strategic about positioning and optimizing your website, your brand can still fare well in these results.

So, let's delve into the details, shall we?

Non-brand visibility is imperative if you wish to reach new customers. By this I mean search queries that do not include your brand name. If Google Analytics tells you most of your organic search is coming from branded keywords, you must do better in answering customers' questions that do not relate to your brand.

So, what is SEO, exactly? SEO (search engine optimization) proactively manages presentation of digital assets (data) with the intent of improving organic search engine visibility. This is not to be confused with search engine marketing, which in industry code means search engine advertising with PPC (pay per click), banners, mobile ads, etc.

Some believe SEO doesn't exist. Some believe SEO is all about manipulation. This used to be true for a segment of the SEO industry using what we call "Black Hat" tactics. Some believe anyone can "do" SEO. However, there truly is an art and science about what makes a website perform well in search.

SEO Secret Sauce

This is one of the biggest secrets to the success of the websites I have optimized. Are you ready?

One of the most powerful ways to reach your customers via organic search on Google, Yahoo!, and Bing is to optimize your digital assets to appeal to your customers during each of the three phases of the purchase decision introduced in chapter 12.

A quick reminder: The 3 Phases of the Purchase Decision:

1. Research

2. Comparison

3. Buy

Let me break this down for you in the context of search. If you are not visible to customers in the Research phase, you may never have the opportunity to compare yourself to competitors or close the sale. You must provide the information customers search for in every phase if you wish to enjoy the full benefit of search. The following is an example of what this would look like for a product, which can be adapted to any brand in any industry.

Research
In the Research phase, a customer might ask, "best suitcase for international travel." Unless they are fiercely loyal to one brand, research queries will not include brand name. Search results may display types of suitcases, recommendations from travel bloggers, or reviews from other travelers on sites that sell suitcases.

Comparison
Once they have determined what type of suitcase they need, customers are likely to conduct another search to compare products and those who sell them. For example, "spinner carryon suitcase" would present results more closely related to a specific product. Additional words like "sturdy," "cheap," "TSA approved," "top rated," or any number of qualifiers could be added to further qualify results. This is why Long Tail SEO becomes extremely effective. Having identified the product they want, customers go on to find the best source for that product.

Purchase
Those who are ready to buy conduct entirely different searches than those in the Research or Comparison phase. They are ready to buy and will do so once their criteria is met. Once they enter the product name, style, color, size, model #, etc. into the search

bar, they will click on the result that appears highest in search that matches their criteria. This is where expertly applied SEO is worth its weight in gold.

A quick note on Google Shopping: Google has recently modified "Shopping" results to include only those who pay to participate in those results. Because products still appear in global search results pages, the decision to participate should be based on how well the brand is competing in organic search and tested for conversion before scaling up as a primary source of traffic.

Search Traffic

How much search engine traffic should your website attract? Having viewed website analytics for numerous sites on a monthly basis over many years, I can tell you that if search engines are not responsible for at least 50 percent of new-visitor traffic, you are losing business to your competitors. Most of my SEO clients over the years have experienced an average of 75 percent of visits via organic search. This continues to evolve as referrals from social media and blogs increase. The actual percentage for each website varies slightly by industry, type of website, content, and can be impacted by seasonal or promotional activities that may include social media, PPC, QR code campaigns, email marketing, etc. A healthy goal is to have organic search account for 50 percent or more of your website traffic.

Search is vital to the success of any website, which is why search must be integrated from the very beginning of website planning throughout the life of the website.

How Important Is Search?

- 94 percent of all clicks go to organic results, as opposed to sponsored results that appear on page 1 of search engine results (Towers, 2012).

- The cost-to-benefit ratio for SEO (search engine optimization) outperforms that of paid search ads, or SEM (search engine marketing). And, although SEO requires maintenance, you are attracting the most qualified clicks (see above) with a lower cost per acquisition over time.

- Search is the first action taken by consumers when they are seeking a product, service, or solution. It has been so for years, and you can expect the same, especially in light of recent integrations between social media and search.

- Google.com is the top destination visited on mobile devices.

- 70 percent of searches on mobile devices result in a conversion or sale within one hour.

Search engine optimization is the best method to proactively leverage your website to reach target audiences via search.

In 2008 I presented these concepts to Internet and technology professionals from Silicon Valley, Asia, Europe, North America, and other places around the world at Web 2.0 in San Francisco. The following are bullets from my presentation, "Integrating SEO, Usability, and Internet Marketing for High Performance and Results," which is just as relevant now as it was then.

Good websites become great when you can:

- Honor the website mission more than the project itself.

- Resist the temptation to use technologically for technology's sake.

- Conduct research to enable strategic positioning to differentiate from competitors.

- Connect left and right sides of the brain to promote readability and usability.

- Proactively integrate search into all phases of the website.

- Challenge old processes and methods to promote nimble response to audience interaction.

- Integrate brand messaging consistently.

- Focus less on the completion of the website and more on performance and ROI.

- Identify what your audience wants and give it to them before competitors do.

- Rely on performance analytics to qualify success and drive future development.

Leverage behavior of loyal customers to guide future evolution and management of the website.

You can view the PowerPoint presentation on SlideShare.com, my LinkedIn profile, or from the book website: MillionDollarWebsite.TV

SEO is not something you slap together or plug in after a website is completed. Effective optimization for search begins at the planning stage, is carried through the website's architecture, and is applied to all digital content, digital assets, and marketing. I have uploaded a copy of this PowerPoint presentation and encourage you review it. It won't take very long, and will introduce you to the foundation of SEO methodology I use every day to effectively serve my clients.

The Rules of SEO

There are no published rules for SEO. What we do have are best practices that the web elite have implemented, tested, tweaked, and analyzed over time to achieve desired results.

I discuss various aspects of SEO throughout the book. I hope you learn something you did not yet know, or perhaps gain confidence in being an informed customer of SEO services. If you embrace this concept about SEO, this book will have paid for itself many times over.

SEO is not an afterthought. It is imperative that search engine optimization reflect the website strategy in planning website architecture, programming, content planning, writing, design, content, image, product and video optimization, RSS content updates, and social media sharing.

As painful as this may be for you to hear, and as angry as the proprietors of many web firms may be with me for saying so, when the vendor you've hired to build your website consumes your website budget and waits until after the website is complete to inform you that SEO was not included, this is website malpractice. Let's make sure you never find yourself in this situation.

SEO Analysis

Because search engine algorithms change frequently and sometimes significantly, I recommend that businesses that are committed to performing in search have an objective SEO analysis conducted. A thorough analysis can be performed by a qualified person within your organization, by one of your vendors, or if you really want to get a fresh perspective, seek out analysis from an independent party. (My firm also provides these audits for clients.)

Before you change a thing, you must evaluate the relationship between your website and search engines. I have created a simple checklist on the website, if you wish to attempt this on your own.

SEO Analysis Checklist

The SEO Analysis Checklist is available for download (for free) from MillionDollarWebsite.TV

This list provides an overview that reveals how compliant the website is with known best practices and various factors that impact search engine performance.

It's worth noting that this list is not representative of all factors known to impact search. Because search engine algorithms are elusive by design, there is no definitive, permanent list of factors from which to create such a checklist. However, I have included the checklist we have adapted over many years, reflecting items that are most frequently overlooked or neglected by website owners, in order to identify strengths and weaknesses that drive the creation of a SEO strategy.

This document on its own will not deliver a detailed SEO prescription for your website. However, the checklist will help you identify the many factors driven from decisions about strategy, architecture, design, content, etc. and gain a better understanding of why SEO should be included from the beginning of the planning process of any website.

SEO Strategy

The web elite know that the SEO strategy must reflect the website strategy. Because I don't have the pleasure of working with you personally through this process, I will walk you through the fundamentals of SEO with the intent of helping you understand what is required so that you may make more informed decisions when it comes to SEO—including selecting who will perform SEO for your website.

SEO requires consistency and diligent implementation of best practices over time. Good SEO is also monitored and continually evaluated and updated using proven optimization methods that respond to new factors as they become part of the search engine landscape.

SEO is most definitely a specialty that requires an in-depth, historical perspective of search engine algorithms, best practices, and an understanding of white hat vs. black hat practices, so as not to jeopardize your site being blacklisted by Google or one of the other search engines.

If you did nothing else beyond applying what I offer you in this chapter, I believe you will be ahead of the curve when it comes to SEO. This is no substitute for professional search engine optimization of your website. However, if you intend to hire an expert, do it yourself, or outsource, this list will help to keep you on track.

SEO Tips:

1. Practice "White Hat" SEO only. Black hat tactics may work temporarily; however, in light of search engine efforts to achieve higher quality results, performance based on spam tactics is typically risky and short-lived. Those who rely upon long-term performance will tell you that black hat SEO is not worth the risk of being blacklisted or punished in a millisecond by the latest Google update or algorithm change by any other search engine.

2. SEO begins with website architecture and includes names of assets in databases, directories, categories of product, product names that will also display as page titles and in URLs, or any other assets that will comprise your website. If you are building a website of 50 pages or less, your site architecture

can likely be organized in a site map. Once you involve dynamic pages driven by databases, legacy data, password-protected data, third-party software, or any external data sources, you will want to consult a website architect to assist the individual responsible for SEO in optimizing all assets. (Don't let them create site architecture without your SEO person; their guidance in the planning phase will likely save you from having to do it twice.)

3. Organize website content thoughtfully. Deliberately plan to qualify content to search engines so they may connect the dots between your website and search engine queries by target audiences. I cannot stress this enough: You must resist the temptation to organize the website to reflect internal departments or how your catalog is printed. Content should be organized according to what serves the customer best, allowing them free and easy access to what they are seeking and what will help them advance from a website visitor to a customer.

4. Use only original content on your website. Even if you are a reseller, distributor, or licensee, duplicate content essentially makes you invisible. Using another's content, even with permission, counts against you in search. Google is especially harsh in calculating duplication of content and essentially deems everything but the most authoritative (typically first to post) invisible. So, invest the time and money necessary to create original content. Here's another tidbit few realize: most brands and manufacturers are not good at writing search-friendly descriptions, so here is your chance to outperform your competition. Write original descriptions and pages for each product according to the guidelines I provide in the chapter on Content and you are sure to see an improvement in visibility. I know, the sheer concept of writing all of that content is overwhelming, especially for retailers that depend upon manufacturers for descriptions. Follow the instructions I provide and I promise it will be worth it.

5. Know your target audience and speak their language, using words THEY use. This is important. In all the years I have been working on websites, I have never worked with a client that understood the relationship between keywords and their customers. It is imperative that you use the words your customers use when presenting your digital assets to the web. This is very difficult for many

organizations that are steeped in industry language, acronyms, proprietary assets, or brands. It is important to associate your digital assets (copy, images, video, FAQs, etc.) with each of the 3 Phases of the shopping experience and use words they are using to Research, Compare, and Purchase your product, solution, service, or concept.

6. Google has moved from "word-based index" to the "Knowledge Graph," and so should you. Instead of stacking keywords (which is against best practice anyway), think about framing content around providing answers to questions and solutions to problems, and become the definitive resource on whatever it is you are in the marketplace to provide. I strongly believe that if you offer what your customers want and can help the search engines determine that you have it, they will do the rest for you.

7. Optimize all website assets even if you think some do not matter right now— search engine algorithms change continuously. This includes all metadata, names of images, alt text, etc. I cannot stress this enough. I do not believe in omitting SEO factors that have ever been considered important. One example is keywords. Some inexperienced SEO practitioners have told clients in recent years not to bother with keywords; however, keywords are often used by some web platforms to generate tags on posts, which do directly impact performance in search. Best practice is to diligently optimize all assets to ensure solid performance over time.

8. Build a "Content Calendar" to schedule the continual update of website content, including RSS feeds and video. This can and should be adapted frequently to proactively "fill the gaps" where you'd like to see the website perform better. You can add pages, posts, videos, testimonials, and other content to elevate relevance for topics that present more competition to reach customers.

9. Avoid linking schemes, pay for link, and link exchanges, including a link to your website vendor. General best practice is to refrain from linking to another website unless it is directly related to the content you offer and is from a respected entity in your industry and/or a more authoritative site than yours. Google has recently punished sites that have built up traffic by a common SEO practice called "link-building." I personally have never believed in this practice

and deliberately did not offer it to our clients. It's a darn good thing too. Many SEO firms that made their living off monthly link-building services have been forced to close shop in the wake of these recent changes by Google.

10. THIS IS IMPORTANT: some website vendors have not caught up with Google's policy on links and still require a link on the home page of their clients' websites within the contract. Make sure your vendor agreement does not include this outdated requirement, or if it is, be sure to omit it before signing on the dotted line. If for any reason there is a link on your website to your vendor, you can and should request the link be removed. If necessary, cite Google's recommendation on links.

11. Forget about PR rating. This rating has had little to do with the performance and profitability of the majority of websites I have worked on for clients. I am not saying a good rating is not desirable—page rank is valuable when calculating the value of incoming links and when justifying quality or value to advertisers, contributors, etc. Page rank is not as relevant to most websites seeking to build a quality experience capable of converting visitors to customers.

12. Do not compare your website to others on resources like Compete.com, Alexa, etc. They do not accurately reflect Internet audiences at large. Most marketers do not know that Alexa requires an opt-in of a tool bar by Internet users, resulting in a very small sample base willing to share their Internet behavior. Additionally, when comparing data on these sources to actual data, webmasters do not find these sources to be accurate in representing "real-world" performance of websites. And, those who do choose to use this data occasionally do so because the portrayal tells a better story than the real data. So, keep this in mind when assessing performance of your own website and that of competitors. Because scoring on these sites is not entirely transparent, it may be difficult to conduct a direct comparison. The best advice is to take data from such sources with a grain of salt.

13. Include "share" functionality on digital assets to enable visitors to share your content. This creates referral visits by way of a type of link that Google

acknowledges. Invite visitors to share pages, posts, videos, infograms, photos, apps, or other assets via email, Twitter, Facebook, Google+, LinkedIn, Reddit, Digg, StumbleUpon, Pinterest, etc. When recipients of the "share" click on the link and visit your website, search engines take notice and include those clicks and visits in search engine algorithms when calculating search engine results.

14. Link your website to your social media profiles, and link your social media profiles to the website. For years now, Google has been extremely proactive in displaying organic search results for brands in search results. When you optimize your social media profiles and link to your website, you are connecting the dots between your social presence and your website for search engines. This becomes highly desirable when your brand is typed into the search bar and page one of search results all go to your website and social profiles. (Who wouldn't want to fill an entire page of search engine results?!)

15. Add the Google+ Badge to your website. This is not to be confused with Google+ Share or a link to your Google+ profile. Google+ Badge is a distinct icon (currently red) that enables Google to verify your identity and connect activity between content such as posts and your profile page. An added bonus for authors is when someone does a Google search on a topic you've written about, your post will appear in results complete with your photo and reference to circles. You will want to learn more about Google Authorship if you plan to write frequently, or across multiple websites. By identifying yourself to Google, your profile appears in search results.

The following image illustrates how "authors" appear in search engine results:

Google | google knowledge graph impacts search forever

Web   Images   Maps   Shopping   More ▾   Search tools

About 3,150,000 results (0.32 seconds)

Google Knowledge Graph Impacts Search and SEO
rebeccamurtagh.com/**google**-**knowledge**-**graph**-influence-o...

by Rebecca Murtagh - in 1,005 Google+ circles - More by Rebecca Murtagh
May 30, 2012 – How **Google Knowledge Graph** Changes **Search** and SEO
Forever. Published ... How Does **Google Knowledge Graph Impact**
Search? Google ...

"Google Knowledge Graph". - Google+
https://plus.**google**.com/+PeteCashmore/.../LXxNTByqiLM

by Pete Cashmore - in 1,579,121 Google+ circles - More by Pete Cashmore
Feb 13, 2012 – Google is building the "**Google Knowledge Graph**". ...
Google Knowledge Graph Could Change **Search Forever** » ... Type in
something like "what is mass **effect** 3 release date" or "How old is bruce willis"
and you will see ...

Google Knowledge Graph And Its Impact On Search Engine Results ...
seo.contentmarketingdigest.com/.../**google**-**knowledge**-**graph**-and-its-...
May 9, 2012 – **Google Knowledge Graph** And Its **Impact** On **Search** Engine Results
. ... Google Adds Explanations To The Knowledge Graph - State of **Search** ..... **Google**
Knowledge Graph Could Change **Search Forever** | SEO Marketing ...

Google's New Medication Knowledge Graph in Search Results ...
sirensong.sireninteractive.com/**google**/**google**s-new-medication-**know**...

16. Note the appearance of the Google Plus Badge on the website in the next
image:

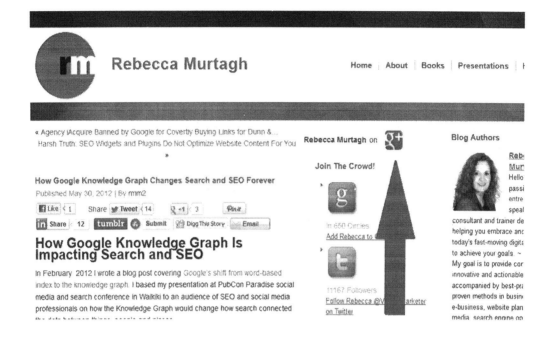

17. Use tools like Google Webmaster Tools, or one of the various professional tools available to monitor site integrity, to ensure your website is crawl-able, is within Google parameters, and all vital assets are present and accounted for. Reports will identify any issues Google identifies with your website, along with enough information to make proactive corrections.

18. Monitor site performance regularly and adapt and adjust to continually improve and sustain optimum search engine visibility. This is typically easier said than done, yet most organizations know when their website is not delivering results such as new visitors, sales or visits to promotions, RSS content, or other assets.

19. Never focus your SEO on 6–12 keywords. This is a huge disservice to your mission and constricts your website's ability to qualify in search. Invest the time and energy to deploy Long Tail SEO which enhances your website's ability to compete and deliver relevant content in context well for a wide variety of keywords and phrases that may be used by your customers in any one of, or all of the 3 Phases of the purchase decision.

20. The more specific your keywords are to each page, the better chance that page has to appear in search engine results and become a landing page. (Clicks to specific landing pages are typically made by far more qualified visitors who are closer to converting themselves from visitor to customer, so optimized landing pages are extremely valuable.)

21. Do not refer to the Google Adwords Keywords Tool or data generated from PPC programs when selecting keywords for organic search engine optimization. Google Adwords is designed to display the keywords worthy of the highest bid and click as they relate to the ads, competitor's ads, and the destination page for each ad. This is quite different from organic search.

22. The power of keywords, even if you are focused on the right keywords, is greatly diminished if you are not search engine optimizing all content. If at all possible, make SEO part of your content-writing and approval process. I cannot stress this enough.

One of my clients is a multi-national consumer brand with whom I have been working with for years. They are so locked into their content development and review process, which includes legal review, that by the time it gets to the website and SEO, the content is untouchable. This means the most important aspect of search engine optimization is off the table. So, we are left using metadata, URLs, and other methods to attempt to qualify the page to the search engines, and we are often prohibited from using the very keywords that would make the page most visible because they are not present in the copy.

Content is the blood that brings life to the body of the website. Without quality content, the site fails to serve as an authoritative destination and business asset capable of supporting business goals. If your process will make delivering quality content challenging, it may be time to evaluate and rethink the sequence in which you produce any and all digital assets.

The Magic of Key Words

The words you choose to communicate your value proposition online will either be your secret sauce or your Achilles heel. It all depends on what words you choose to focus on and how you use them.

The first word of advice I can offer you is to fire your SEO service provider if they ask you to provide a keyword list. I know this may sound harsh, but I feel very strongly about this, as do those who understand search from a mature perspective.

Keywords are essential to achieving visibility of any website. And, believe it or not, it doesn't matter what industry you are in, every day a potential customer conducts searches on the Internet to Research, Compare, or Purchase a solution to a problem. Even if they met a representative of your organization offline, chances are very good that they will visit your website. After all, what's the first thing you do when you hear about a new product or company? You Google it, or conduct a search of course!

If you are visible, you have a chance to provide that solution, to win a new customer. If you are not visible, your competitors probably are and they will have the honor of entertaining the new business that could have been yours.

A majority of Internet users use multiple words to refine search results. Aside from seeking a specific brand (which is typically one word), most keyword searches include more than one keyword. In fact, the average length of a search engine query has gotten longer over time. And, the more keywords they use, the more qualified the click is likely to be.

A website has much to gain when it achieves visibility to the most qualified visitors. Search engine optimization leverages the relationship between keywords and phrases to resonate with target audiences. One of the most effective methods to expand your reach to new customers in search is to help your website qualify for a multitude of keyword queries. You can achieve this quite effectively through Long Tail SEO. Long Tail introduces many words and phrases to express concepts in multiple ways to make it more relevant to the many ways humans search.

Remember the 3 Phases of the Purchase Cycle? Long Tail SEO is a highly effective method of optimizing content to reach customers in any one, or all of the three phases: Research, Compare, and Purchase.

Let's say a consumer is searching for a hotel in Dallas, Texas. This will produce a number of results, of course. As they view results in the initial Research phase, they begin to define the criteria that will best meet their needs. Those ready to advance to the Comparison phase use the criteria to narrow results to include the most qualified of the results. From there, the decision to book (Purchase) will be made.

In doing so, we may use qualifiers to hone in on hotels that will meet our criteria. This could be smoke-free, affordable, highly rated, and close to the airport. Another person might conduct a search with the same intent using words such as non-smoking, cheap, best rated, airport shuttle—you get the general idea. Yet, another search might use the words non-smoking, best reviews, and airport business hotel. You see, there are many ways to conduct the same search. Long Tail would introduce these variations throughout the assets presented, including but not limited to pages, posts, images, videos, etc.

Who Wins the Click?

Achieving top position in organic search results is just the beginning of effective SEO. After all, what good is being #1 if your ideal customers are not clicking? How well you optimize your digital assets could determine whether the click comes to your website or that of your competitor.

Pre-qualifying the Click

What appears in search results is vitally important when competing for the click. It is highly likely the prospect will return to their search results unless they do not find what they are looking for. You have one opportunity to win the click.

The right message displayed in the #3 search result can win over the click from the #1 or #2 results in search, which will likely contribute to a higher ranking over time.

Metadata is still displayed (and highlighted) in search engine results pages (SRPs). However, because Google has stated that it will bypass meta descriptions to extrapolate more relevant content or data, optimization of each page and the website in its entirety is vital to realizing optimum performance in search.

You can compete more directly in search with metadata and related page content that is optimized to educate (phase 1), differentiate from competitors (phase 2), and present a compelling offer to promote conversion (phase 3).

One of the most effective ways to get a qualified visitor to your website is through qualified landing pages. Search engines will deliver your customer to the page that most closely relates to the customer's query when they can find it. You can elevate the effectiveness of your landing pages by optimizing them for search visibility and conversion. The web elite understand the imperative to ensure visitors can find everything they need to convert themselves from a visitor to a customer from any landing page within the website.

This is why it is imperative to make secondary and tertiary pages qualified for search. You cannot optimize the home page and a few secondary pages and expect the site to achieve the same results as could be expected if the entire site was optimized for visibility, clicks, and conversion.

Introducing content in context of the Research, Comparison, and Purchase phases of the customer decision process enables search engines to deliver content most relevant to that customer, wherever that customer is in the process at that moment.

Here's an example:

You are seeking an automotive mechanic to provide an inspection and oil change that won't interfere with your busy schedule. Which would you be more likely to click on?

URLs and samples are intended to be fictitious and used for illustrative purposes only. "Mytown" could be replaced with the name of any town or city.

Mytown Automotive Shop
All Makes and Models. Call for an appointment.
http://smithsautoshop.com

Mytown Convenient Certified Auto Mechanics
ASE Certified Automotive Mechanics. Convenient hours 7am-6pm, 7 days a week. We guarantee our work. No Appointment Necessary for Inspections and Oil Changes.
http://mytownautomechanics.com

Bob's Automotive Shop
1520 Main street, Mytown, USA, (555) 555-1212 , Bob Smith opened his shop in 2009. Tune-ups, maintenance, tire sales and installation, oil and filter changes.
http://smithsautoshop.com

Relevance and Authority

Search engines now care about more than what is on your website. Because they are in the business of delivering the most qualified results to answer a search query, they take relevance and authority into account when determining which results will appear in the #1, #2, #3 position, etc.

You will have some control over relevance. In search, relevance is all about how closely you talk about the problem your organization is out to solve, including how closely your website content matches your customers' searches. The more they click, the more relevant your content is, the higher Google perceives the quality of your content to be.

Authority is a bit more complicated because it relies upon the interaction of others. Authority reflects how trusted your website and brand are to your audiences and peers. Authority is influenced by referrals (links to your content), mentions on other websites (which also hopefully includes links to your website), social media "likes," "follows," "fans," and shares.

Because social interaction is now part of the search engine algorithms of Google, Yahoo!, and Bing, you must take advantage of every possible way the search engines can make a connection to your brand, and back to your website.

Your Brand & SEO

Appearing at the top of search engine results for your brand is imperative. A brand could be the name of your company, marquee product, organization, a character, or even your social media handle. Your brand should dominate page one search results with your website, social media profiles, blog posts, and media coverage. If it doesn't, you need to get busy and optimize every digital asset you own.

Unfortunately, appearing #1 in search for your brand is not an indication that your website is search engine optimized. Why? Because only those who have purchased from you before, already visited your website, read about you, or referred to you, will use your brand to conduct a search. If you are unable to compete in searches that exclude your brand, you will be unable to compete for new visitors and customers. If you consider the 80/20 rule of Long Tail, your brand should be in 20 percent of your search engine traffic, and the remaining 80 percent should arrive on your website using keywords related to solving the problem and differentiating yourself from your competitors. Hopefully you recognize these as customers in the Research and Comparison phases we discussed in chapter 12; "3 Phases of the Purchase Decision".

Let me illustrate this with an example:

Let's say the name of your company is Acme and you sell widgets. Ideally, 20 percent of search engine traffic would find your website using the word "Acme" and 80 percent would not include the word "Acme" but would include many variations of keywords and phrases that solve the customer's problem and differentiate you from the competition. Phrases like "widgets made in USA," "waterproof widgets," "widget custom colors," "widgets free shipping," "widget sale," "widget reviews," and so on.

Long Tail SEO

Long tail SEO (of which I am a very strong advocate) requires a multi-tier keyword strategy that is applied uniquely to each page while supporting the overall mission of the website. When done properly, SEO should enable visitors to find your website or specific landing pages using dozens, hundreds, thousands, even tens or hundreds of thousands of keywords and phrases.

The concept of Long Tail was introduced to the marketing and Internet world by *Wired* magazine editor Chris Anderson back in October 2004. He later authored the book *Long Tail, the Revised and Updated Edition: Why the Future of Business is Selling Less of More*, which essentially turns the 80/20 rule (also known as Pareto's distribution principle) on its ear, at least when it comes to the reliance of keywords for search engine marketing to generate results.

The 80/20 Rule

Essentially, if we apply the concept to SEO and keywords, Long Tail means that instead of the 20 percent of keywords generating 80 percent of the clicks or business, 80 percent of less dominant keywords, implemented as phrases that reach a broader mass, can actually achieve better results, reflecting how the American economy is shifting from mass market to millions of niches. Knowing your niche and reaching out to it effectively via search is the essence of Long Tail SEO.

In all the years I have performed search engine optimization, I have yet to meet a client focusing on the right keywords. Take the time to find an expert that TRULY understands the relationship between content, keywords, and your customers—they are worth their weight in gold.

Think like Your Customers

Keywords must resonate with your customers, so resist the temptation to rely solely upon the words you use to describe your brand, product, and/or services. Think about the problem you are solving because that is most likely how your customers are searching—it's even how you are searching.

When you are looking for accommodations in a place you've never visited, you most likely begin with a search that includes the name of the location and phrases like "best hotels," "hotel with bar," "romantic bed and breakfast," "hotel near airport," etc. These qualifiers reduce the number of results and display the websites that more closely match the query.

For example, if you search for "seo training" on Google, over 30 million results are found. As you conduct more research and become more educated, you may determine that you need "white hat" or "long tail SEO," and add them to your search. Doing so not only narrows the results to a range of 230,000 to 734,000 results, depending on which combination of words you use, it also identifies websites offering exactly what you are looking for.

Natural Language

Using real-world language goes a long way in search engine optimization. And, because there are SO many ways to say something, the more creatively you can look at your keywords, the better they are likely to perform for you.

An American seeking hotel accommodation in Roma, Italy, might search for:

- Rome hotels

- Best hotels in Rome

- English-speaking hotels

- Best hotel in Rome for Americans

- Best-rated Rome hotel by Americans

- Hotel catering to English-speaking guests

- Best Rome hotels for English-speaking travelers

- Best Rome hotels for families

- Most romantic hotel in Rome

- Rome hotels with views

- Rome hotels near public transportation

- Rome hotels near Coliseum

As a general rule, the more defined the search, the more qualified the click.

The Search for Reviews

When seeking a product, a search often includes the word "reviews," so be sure to include it in your SEO strategy, as well as a page that will qualify as a landing page if you don't include reviews beside each product.

Link Building

Most SEO services will include optimization of your website, which I have previously outlined. Many SEO firms will also sell you on "link-building services." However, as I've said, if you build quality content, your website will not require a link-building scheme. This is a very controversial topic in my industry, and I've had many discussions, even heated debates, over the topic of link-building.

My position is that when you publish quality, relevant content, those with credible websites will link to your content on its own merit, creating far more superior referrals than you could buy in structured "link-building" programs that the search engines can recognize. It's all about Authority and Reputation, and the more legitimate the link, the more powerful the "juice" you get from their link to your content.

SEO firms who depend on the sale of sell link-building services vehemently disagree with this theory, largely because their on-page SEO methods are unsuccessful in achieving top position for clients.

I recall a rather heated discussion with the owner of an SEO firm in the Dallas, Texas, area at a networking event where she was nearly arguing with me that top position on Google was simply impossible without link-building. I told her it was indeed possible and that in all the years I'd been doing SEO I had never sold link-building programs, and instead focused on creating quality content to attract links from unsolicited referrals. She all but called me a liar. Then, she called over her technologist and repeated my claim, seeking his confirmation that I could not possibly be telling the truth. Much to her amazement, he backed me up, saying "It's possible if you really know what you are doing—difficult—but doable." I suspect they went back to the office so that she could ask him why they were not deploying such methods, but that's pure speculation.

I have, indeed, achieved top Google positions—#1, #2, and/or #3—for client websites for multiple keywords and phrases consistently over the years without deploying a link-building program.

Google recently began penalizing for various link-building schemes. So if you are still tempted or sold on the link-building practice to build up search visibility, do your homework, know who you are working with, and be prepared to make adjustments in light of any further search engine algorithm changes.

Social Media and Search

I would be remiss if I didn't mention the increasingly intense relationship between social media and search. In 2009, social media became part of the search engine scene. Because I am continually observing and testing, we recognized this relationship long before the industry caught on. In fact, I led my team in testing the relationship between Google and Twitter, which led to us being able to create page one search results for social media profiles a full nine months before it was formally announced by Google. In 2011, the relationship between Google and Twitter ceased as Google ramped up to launch Google Plus. Google+ is, of course, Google's social platform of choice, creating several opportunities to leverage social media in search to improve visibility of your website and the content within.

Social Media Is a Vital Part of Your Search and Visibility Strategy

If you would like to learn more about this topic, you can hear me speak about this topic at events like Pubcon in Las Vegas or Hawaii, Digital World Expo, follow me on Twitter @VirtualMarketer, circle me on Google+ (as Rebecca Murtagh), watch for my upcoming book *Spheres of Influence*, or attend one of my workshops or seminars on the topic.

So, if visibility requires SEO and search is so complex, what can you do to make it an effective part of your website strategy? There are several approaches I could recommend to enable you to achieve the results you seek.

- Seek guidance from a search engine optimization expert (someone who is a recognized expert in their field, or recommended by someone you know and trust).

- Hire an SEO copywriter to optimize your website content before it becomes final.

Website Vendor Links

Remember, the best link is a link generated naturally to share your content with new audiences. Never, Never, Never include a link to your webmaster, web designer, new media firm, or web developer on the bottom of the home page of your website.

Back in the early days, this was very common practice. Over recent years, however, this has become a practice that benefits the vendor at the expense of their clients. Often, this link is inserted into the terms of the agreement and automatically added to every website they create. It is incumbent upon you to eliminate this requirement. And, if a link to the vendor is already there, remove it. Here's why:

Over the years, SEO practitioners have speculated on where Google stood on the use of links. However, in 2012, Google came out and stated that link incentives are a form of trade and payment and make for unnatural links for the purpose of manipulating page rank, which is against Google Webmaster guidelines.

Link Exchange or Building Programs

Google harshly punished those deploying deliberate linking schemes to connect the dots to their website(s) with the Penguin Update in May 2012. Since that time, Google has also stated that requiring, posting, or requesting links in exchange for something goes against Google Webmaster Guidelines meaning you should avoid doing so if you wish Google to view links on your website properties favorably. In fact, Google banned an agency for their role in soliciting links for one of their clients. To learn more about how Google made an example of one agency for buying links, visit: MillionDollarWebsites.TV

Search Goes Beyond The Website

Search engines are everywhere. Search function exists on websites, social media platforms, directories, and various other web platforms. How well you optimize owned digital assets will directly impact how easy it will be for your ideal customers to find what they are looking for, the way you want them to find it. Optimization of social profiles, updates, uploads comments on other websites, forums and blogs can greatly improve the visibility of those efforts.

Video, Images, News, Blogs and More (Oh My!)

Copy and content are not the only owned assets you should be optimizing. SEO applies to video, images, press releases, promotions, blog posts, and just about anything else you add to the web. Whether you are posting on your own website, or a platform owned by someone else like YouTube, Instagram, Pinterest, PR Distribution Websites, etc., optimization may determine whether anyone else ever sees what you upload. Be sure to name the file and utilize Alt text and other descriptive fields to make the item more visible to those who will find it of value.

Clean Code

Many Do-It-Yourself webmasters and small businesses overlook some of the more technical aspects of the website, which can have a direct impact on search engine performance, usability, and conversion. This is understandable as technical knowledge is often required to correct any issues.

Over the past couple of years, Google has made it increasingly easy for organizations of all sizes to know exactly how well their website is performing by offering Google Webmaster Tools. This free platform is separate from Google Analytics and offers valuable insight every website owner and webmaster will value. Implementation requires a simple ownership verification process. Webmaster tools can and should be live for every website you own.

I find Google Webmaster Tools invaluable in providing performance insight when evaluating and making recommendations for optimization of website SEO, usability, design, and conversion. Reports identify code, page load, and 404 errors that can be used to improve performance that will directly impact search engine performance, time on the website, bounce rates, and conversion.

There are many other reports, such as crawl errors, last date indexed, etc. that reveal the performance and compliance of various website factors to best practices and Google's rules for search.

Text to Code Ratio

The basic premise behind this is that you don't want the data in your website. Defining your goals and aligning in-house and external resources will enable you to identify the team members best qualified to support your goals, which will help you prioritize investment in each area of the website.

Meet Them Where They Are

Your website, video channel, social media profiles, updates, listing on directories, review sites, mentions in blogs, and your own blog have become an integral part of search—not only on their own merit, but also as a reflection of how much authority your brand has. Social queues are now part of search engine algorithms, which take into account the reach of your brand as well as the sentiment of that reach. The more your audiences like you, the more search engines do.

What Would Google Do?

If you were a search engine, which of the two websites would you perceive to have more authority?

Notice this website, typical of a high-performing website in 2008, has pages and posts (RSS), as well as a Facebook and Twitter page. Many websites at this time did not have RSS, or social media connections. And, many still lack these basic owned assets.

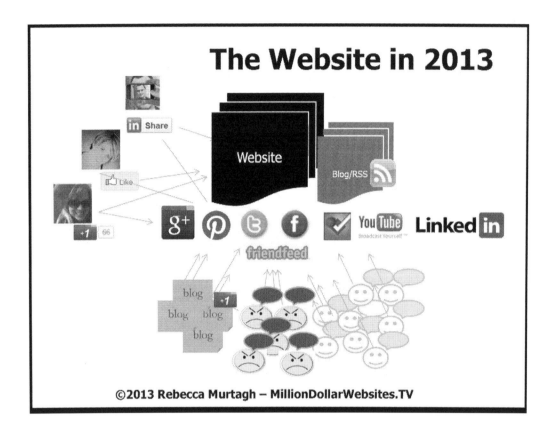

This is how a strategically-deployed website might appear to search engines in 2013. Notice the interaction between owned assets (pages, posts and social profiles), with interaction with people on platforms the brand has profiles, as well as other platforms where customers actively share and interact with the brand.

The more engaged your brand is with others on the web, the greater your authority. The search engines care about what is being said about your brand as much they care about the intensity and volume of mentions. One retailer learned this the hard way. He continually ranked at the top of search, not because he was the best in town but because he was the worst in town and was enjoying top search position because of the sheer volume of complaints about his store. Once Google updated their algorithm to parse negative sentiment from positive sentiment, he lost the position in search.

Search Is No Longer Just about SEO

SEO (search engine optimization) used to be defined as the optimization of website assets. Then came the authority of links, the power of Web 2.0 content, RSS, and the list goes on. Today, SEO requires a holistic approach to ALL digital assets, including websites, blogs, video channels, catalogs, and yes, social media.

Millions of searches are conducted every day on Google, Bing, and Yahoo!. But it doesn't stop there. Search is conducted on YouTube, Google+, Twitter, Linkedin, Facebook, Yelp, Tripadvisor, OpenTable, Instagram, Pinterest, and countless other digital destinations.

Before you begin to think that having a website is a popularity contest, let's put it all in perspective with another reference to our youth. You aren't seeking votes for homecoming king or queen (or maybe you are); you are working to be king of the hill.

It Is Good to Be King

Just like the game King of the Hill, rest assured the moment you overcome your competition to achieve top position, competing brands will seek to take you down. Maybe the king you replaced will be fighting to win back the hill. The same is true in search. The moment you dominate visibility, you will have a target on your back. Your competition will not stand by and watch you get the lion's share of new customers. There is too much at stake. Just as you want to be #1, so do they. SEO requires ongoing maintenance, which we cover again later in the book.

Chapter 14:

Conversion

You don't have to be in the retail business to seek a conversion or sale. A conversion can be qualified as a purchase, enrollment, opt-in, review, "like," download, sharing, registration, attendance, call, form submission, or demo. Your website must be prepared to invite visitors to become customers.

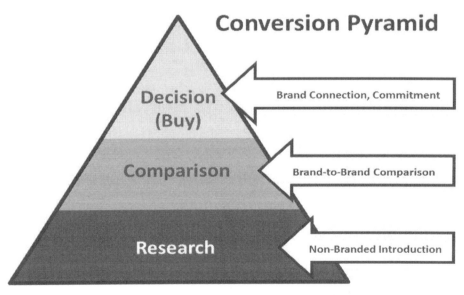

Conversion Pyramid

- Decision (Buy) — Brand Connection, Commitment
- Comparison — Brand-to-Brand Comparison
- Research — Non-Branded Introduction

© 2012 MillionDollarWebsite.TV

Customers Pre-Qualify Themselves

Making every piece of decision-related content accessible to your customers is paramount. You should be prepared to answer questions, overcome objections, and differentiate your brand from competitors for each of the personas you created to represent your customers. The more proactively you do this on pages and posts of your website, the more visible your brand becomes in search to customers in the Research, Comparison, or Purchase phase of their decision.

The 3-Click Rule

When it comes to planning site architecture, content organization, and building the site map, you want to make sure that no piece of content is ever more than three clicks away from the home page. Making it easy for visitors to find the information they need to pre-qualify themselves, research options, compare solutions, and step up to become a viable customer or lead through the organization, writing, and optimization of content should always be the filter by which you review every phase of the website.

The accessibility of content is covered in several chapters of this book. For the purpose of conversion, remember that it is imperative that each customer type (persona) be able to create their own path to conversion. This objective will influence architecture, content organization, website design, usability, SEO, links to and from content, and calls to action. Don't forget to consider features such as Q&A, live chat, customer support, and transactions to convert the visitor to a customer.

The One-Click Proposition

Unlike the 3-Click Rule for content, there should be some call to action, or invitation for conversion should be clickable from each and every page of your website. Somehow, somewhere, it is imperative that you make conversion a one-click proposition.

Measuring Conversion

Use website goals, personas and KPIs to define requirements and validate the investment made in the website. These guidelines will also help to identify any additional efforts required to achieve organizational goals, such as SEO, social media integration, online catalog enhancement, media room, etc.

Also, use analytics and reporting tools to quantify conversions for each audience to enable reporting. This can be achieved in free programs such as Google Analytics, as well as other website reporting platforms.

Chapter 15:

Site Architecture and Organization of Digital Assets

I understand. For many, this aspect of the website is not fun, sexy, or interesting. However, I have to tell you this one step transforms your website strategy into a blueprint that can be interpreted and followed by others, keeping everyone's eye on the ball—the same ball.

Whether you are communicating your objectives to your in-house team, outsourced vendors, or taking on the website yourself, implementing this phase into the website planning process has saved so many of my clients time and money, creating a greater margin for performance, ROI, and profitability.

Site Architecture

"Information Architecture" is terminology often used for sites that will be professionally developed. I was first introduced to website architecture in the 1990s while working alongside IT professionals. I have been extremely fortunate to have worked with extremely intelligent and creative software architects. Of course, they weren't called that in the day. They were engineering and software graduates of some of the nation's most prestigious colleges and universities who also found themselves drawn to the Internet. As they created "shopping carts" for online transactions long before they were called shopping carts and SAAS applications before the acronym had been adopted, they graciously answered my questions and indulged my ideas on how to create solutions and services that clients would value enough to pay for, which was especially challenging when the commercial Internet was still in its infancy.

All It Takes Is One Bad Apple or Character

What I have learned from the brilliant minds of IT, software, architecture, and engineering, is that good structure and planning are vital to the creation of a successful product. One bad line of code could destroy months of work. The same is true for a website, the bridge between technology, marketing, and people—your people … customers.

Doors That Don't Open

The last thing you want to do is confuse your customers or invite them to do something on your website that you are unable to support. Failing to deliver what you have led your customers to expect from you and your website is likely to frustrate visitors. Think about what Mrs. Winchester did with her crazy configuration of stairs that led to the ceiling, doors that went nowhere, and windows that opened only to another room in the house. If you have ever been to the Winchester house in San Jose, California, you have experienced this firsthand. Just being in the house is frustrating. That is exactly how web visitors feel when they can't find what they want or expect from a website. Luckily, it doesn't have to be this way. As they said when they built the Six Million Dollar Man: "We have the technology" to do better, so we must do just that.

Think of Templates and Themes as Suggestions

Even if you decide a template, theme, or software program is the method you will use to build your website, it is never a good idea to use a cookie cutter approach to build a website (unless of course you are the website firm seeking high profit margins). Instead, think of templates and themes as mere suggestions, a framework from which to build your own environment.

The website structure should uniquely reflect your brand, assets, and the path needed to convert visitors to customers. Your website may or may not include complex mapping of custom programming, scripts, integration of legacy software, real-time data sources, or membership databases. Even if your website is as small as 10 pages, you must methodically plan how those pages will be presented and how visitors will be lead to access them if you wish to reap the rewards of a quality website.

It's Only Human

Always remember that a human is accessing the website without your assistance or guidance. Oddly enough, many get so wrapped up in meeting the requirements of their organization that they forget that the website is designed to serve the needs of humans, one visit at a time.

The Simplest Website Benefits from Information Architecture (IA)

We do not have the time or space to get into the technical methods inherent to information architecture, nor do we need to for you to participate in the technology planning process. Besides, I promised you would not have to learn to speak a new language to master the website process. So, we will explore some of the most scalable practices to help you proactively lead the discussion on the architecture of a websites of any scale.

Just as you must first construct the foundation of a home or office building before building up the walls, defining spaces, and then filling those spaces with fixtures, decorations, and furniture, you must define function. After all, you wouldn't want plumbing to come up through the middle of the dining room to reach the second-floor bath would you?

Website architecture can be represented by schemas, site maps, and site designs. Each of these represents a different presentation of how the website will work. I'll boil these down to the simplest terms to illustrate what they are and how they contribute to the planning of the website.

The Schema

The schema works out the details of how assets on your website will interact with data sources and software and how it will dynamically generate displays of that data. For example, if you have a zip code search on your website, this feature would require interaction with a database to display a results page. The source of this data as well as how and where the website translates the query to display results is represented in the schema. The schema often represents actions that are seemingly invisible to the website visitor, yet often represents interactivity that differentiates one website from another.

Schemas are typically prepared by the lead architect or programmer for the website in collaboration with the individual(s) leading the planning of the website (that's you!). You do not have to be technologically advanced to create the site map to communicate the desired relationship between back-end data and applications with publicly-displayed assets that will create the user experience on the website, from which a full schema can be generated

When you work with experienced professionals, you can invite them to make recommendations that will further enable you to clarify and define the user experience according to your website strategy and mission. You can see why it is imperative that the strategy and mission be complete before entering these discussions.

The following is a sample schema, just to give you an idea of how they reflect the exchange and organization of data.

Planning Tools

Mapping architecture for a website can be achieved on paper or a whiteboard. However, it is difficult to send one of those to a vendor through email. So, even if you start with the hand-drawn approach, it is wise to replicate website architecture in digital format. Mind-mapping software can be used to achieve this, and there are many available. I'd suggest a Google search to find a few that appeal to you and give them a try. Or, you can keep it simple and use Microsoft PowerPoint, Word, Visio, Adobe Photoshop, or Illustrator.

The Site Map

The Site Map is the road map for your website and should be part of every RFP, design meeting, programmer meeting, SEO, and content plan. The Site Map should continue as a guiding document as you build your Content Calendar and manage the addition of assets over time. No website should be built without this document, but if I had a dollar for every website that went live without a site map, I would be very, very wealthy today.

So why is a site map so valuable? The site map is the precursor to the website design, prioritizes the presentation of content and assets according to your strategy, and enables the mechanics of the website to be approached methodically, rather than randomly.

I am often shocked to see how many websites present every page of the site as equal in importance. This not only makes it difficult for visitors to explore the website, but it works against the organization that search engines seek when qualifying your content as landing pages in search engine results. We discuss landing pages further in the chapter on SEO.

Buckets of Information

The site should present "buckets" of information that relate to how you meet the needs of visitors and how doing so supports your goal to convert visitors to customers. This makes it far easier for visitors to explore the content most relevant to them, and the organization of content helps search engines identify and present that content in results for related searches.

The following Site Map samples illustrate how the site map is used to organize digital assets, which can then be used to guide website design, content, SEO, usability, advertising, and conversion.

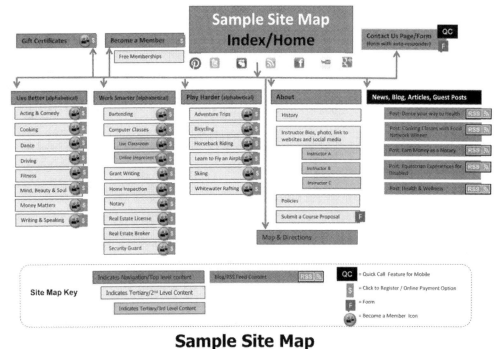

Sample Site Map

For more on how to use Site Maps to plan and build a winning website, refer to the book:
Million Dollar Websites by Rebecca Murtagh
Visit MillionDollarWebsite.tv

Learn more about the website site map on the website: MillionDollarWebsite.TV

This sample site map effectively organizes digital assets into "buckets" of information that have been created to engage visitors based on their interest.

Top level pages, which are accessible in primary navigation, are identified as accessible from the home/index page. Because visitors can arrive on any one of the assets on the website in a multitude of ways (search, email, advertising, social media, etc.), these pages are typically available from any page or post on the website through the primary navigation.

Secondary pages (second level) and tertiary pages (third level) are also reflected in the previous site map. A fourth level (quaternary pages) can also be added, should you determine placement of content at that level is required. Just be careful not to go too "deep" with content; the deeper content is buried, the less likely users and search engines are likely to find it. However, this fourth level can be useful in creating destination pages for limited distribution email, exclusive promotion offers, etc. (not to be confused with public offers, promotions and invitations for all visitors, which should be front and center via RSS or design at the highest levels of the website). Fourth-level pages may still be found by others but do not interrupt the flow of the user experience for the masses.

Calls to action are identified by icons. For example, "click to call" for mobile, online registration, become a member, and forms are placed on specific pages to promote the conversion of visitors to customers. Social media share icons and profile links are also represented to ensure they are integrated into the site planning and design discussions.

In the next illustration you will see the same site map without the icons representing calls to action. This is where many stop in the site map process. As you can see, by comparing this example with the previous site map, this "unplugged" version of the site map falls short of telling the full story of how the website will use digital assets presented to support goals (CONVERSION!).

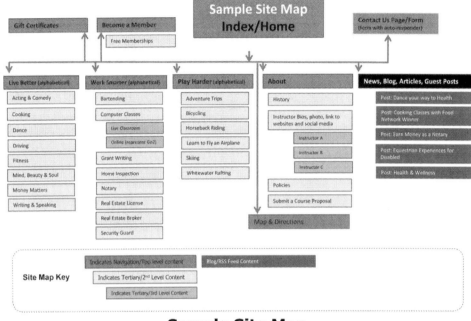

Sample Site Map

For more on how to use Site Maps to plan and build a winning website, refer to the book:
Million Dollar Websites **by Rebecca Murtagh**
Visit MillionDollarWebsite.tv

Tips for Creating a Website Site Map

Hierarchy Rules

An organized website makes the user experience easier to build, optimize, and manage over time. But there is more. When you approach the content and assets of your website within a hierarchy, you improve the relationship of assets, making it easier for your customers and search engines to find.

It is also much easier to build a Content Calendar, link promotions to product or service pages, reference static pages from posts, and promote exploration of the site no matter how the visitor arrives when the site is organized and all parties involved are working from the same sheet of music—your site map!

Home Is Where the Heart Is

The heart and soul of your website is your home page. It is often the very first interaction others have with your brand. It is also the launching point of the user experience, where search engines often deliver visitors by default, and the place that users will return to start again when they've lost their way and want to start over or explore other options on your website.

As you can see from the last example, a site map is like building a house upside down.

Website content organization is much like the outlines you created for book reports when you were in grade school. In fact you can even begin outlining your website in outline form and translate it to a site map once you have worked out the details.

Now let's walk through the four levels of websites and how they can be used strategically.

The home page is considered the foundation or anchor from which all assets flow. From there you should be able to access all primary "buckets" of content and assets, which should also be reflected in permanent, primary navigation.

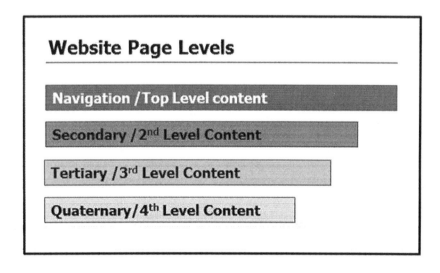

Secondary pages can also be considered containers of content when you are going to include tertiary or quaternary pages. As such, secondary pages become the framework to organize supporting content within each bucket.

A word of caution: one of the biggest mistakes you can make is to make every page of your website a secondary page. This essentially presents all content as equal in importance to visitors and search engines. A "flat" website that presents every page as equal in importance creates several challenges. When you do not prioritize pages and digital assets, website visitors are less likely to easily access products, solutions, or information that should reside with similar content. So, to spread it all out is like placing every page of this book flat on the floor and attempting to find one page of specific content. This approach discourages exploration and may even turn visitors away from the website. Remember, you have only two to three seconds from the moment visitors arrive on the website before they determine their next course of action. Will they leave or will they stay?

Mapping the Future

In addition to promoting a user-friendly experience today, the site map you create will also serve as a guide for all content to be added in the future. The more organized your website is, the easier it is to build upon it over time without having to build a new website or redesign the user experience. Using the map to add content over time (pages, posts, video, documents, etc.) is mission critical when it comes to adding value, building authority, and qualifying for search.

Scalability

As your business grows, so must your website, and vice-versa. When you are strategic in mapping out and building an online environment that meets the needs of your customers and supports your bottom line, your website should naturally be scalable.

Your Website Is Scalable If...

- The website is built on a platform that includes a CMS (content management system) that allows you to manage content in real time.

- The website site map organizes assets to facilitate easy and strategic additions to your offering—products, services, profiles, members, downloads, etc.

- Accepting a conversion can be supported by more than one person and more can be added as needed (fulfillment, proposals, billing, etc.).

- It is possible to add pages, posts, video, images, etc. without having to hire a vendor and without additional cost.

- Your website host, designer, or developer does not limit how many pages or posts you can add to your website.

- Your business is prepared to meet and fulfill the demands of website visitors.

… which leads us to perhaps the most important topic of this entire book—being prepared for success, which we cover in Chapter 25.

Posts

RSS = Really Simple Syndication

Folks seem to have a hard time grasping the difference between static pages and posts from an RSS feed. The difference is simple.

Pages are fixed assets on your website with a permanent placement within the website structure. They reside at a designated location and are accessed via navigation.

Posts are slightly different in that they are part of a feed, can be added quickly, and do not interfere with website navigation. An added benefit to posts is that when the website is set up properly, every addition to the RSS feed generates a notification to search engines, making your site more visible via search (especially when your posts are optimized).

You have the option of making posts open for comments, holding comments for moderation before they go live, and opting in or out on making posts eligible for trackbacks and pingbacks. Wordpress.org offers a deeper explanation of these features.

View Your RSS Feed

If you have a blog or have used RSS functionality to post news, press releases, events, or other time-sensitive posts, your content is part of a feed. Your website's RSS feed should be visible by visiting the primary page for RSS content, which can typically be viewed by adding "/feed" at the end of the URL.

For example, when you visit my website RebeccaMurtagh.com, you see posts because I have elected to make posts the primary content of the website rather than static pages. To view the feed, you would visit: RebeccaMurtagh.com/feed

Why do you care about having a feed? Because your feed is the mechanism by which you can push your posts out to others, via an RSS reader or inclusion on other websites. For example, I include my feed on my LinkedIn profile so that every time I add a new post, it automatically populates on LinkedIn. This is just one example of how your RSS feed can be used to introduce your content to new audiences.

Search Engines Treat Pages and Posts Differently

Worthy of mention is that search engines crawl pages and posts differently. It can take many hours, days, weeks, or months for Google, Yahoo!, and Bing to find, index, and include a website page in search engine results. Posts, on the other hand, can be viewed in search results within minutes when created, presented, and optimized properly.

RSS content should be represented on your site map, schema (when driven by other data sources), and design. RSS content is content that generates a feed that can be populated by blog posts, news, promotions, press releases, and other content, and it can also become the entry point to your website. Because these will be added over time, the best approach for now is to represent the landing page and categories. For example, if you plan to share tips, industry news, and press releases, you want to create three categories for RSS content, which identifies which category you would assign new posts to. Categories can easily be added. Posts should be a primary focus of a Content Calendar, and the addition of new content should be scheduled strategically to improve visibility in search, support promotions, serve as a destination for social media interaction, and engage users over time.

Bread Crumbs

Because website visitors can arrive on your website from a variety of entry points, such as search, email, advertisements, social media shares, etc., you want to ensure that core navigation, presentation of information, and calls to action vital to conversion are ever present. Primary navigation is mentioned in the context of website design in the earliest stages because this impacts usability, SEO, time on the website, clicks, and conversion. After all, you aren't building a website to simply paint a pretty picture of your business; you expect your website to serve a purpose.

What's that? You didn't think SEO had anything to do with design? Not to worry, this is a common misconception. We will explore this in greater depth, but for now I want to make sure SEO is on your radar when considering website design.

The website design should specifically identify website navigation, multimedia features, text, video and images, as well as the language or platform that will be used to deliver said assets. This is an extremely important phase of the website process. Design choices significantly impact how well website visitors find and interact with your website. If you build a home page dependent upon Java, your load time will increase significantly. If you build a site from Flash, or feature Flash, some or all of your content will not be visible on Apple mobile devices, and Google has announced they will no longer support Flash on Android mobile devices. You must consider these issues before investing in website design. We explore best practices in website design further in the chapter on High Performance Website Design.

Time Waits for No One

One of the most unique aspects of the website is that unlike a building, bridge, or software, the environment in which the website must perform is extremely fluid and changes every second of every day, often in unexpected ways. Whether the time between the launch of the website plan and the moment the website goes live is days, weeks, or months, the landscape in which that website must compete and perform will have changed.

Factors such as search engine visibility, user preferences, browser updates, hosting, usability, and device usage change the way your customers and website visitors find and consume the experience you build. These factors directly impact how well your website delivers the results you seek. Integrating checks and balances into your website plan enables you to assess and adapt to emerging trends in usage. This is even more powerful when you have your ear to the ground. Real-time access to website analytics of your current website provides invaluable insight into how the latest shift in the environment influences your audience's interaction with your content and digital assets, enabling you to adapt the plan along the way, defining phased improvements where warranted.

Prepare for the Worst, Hope for the Best

Just as you would architect a building, bridge, or software to endure environmental influences, as well as internal and external threats and emergencies, the website requires a similar approach. The face of these may be different, but the impact can be equally devastating if you are not prepared. Just as you define the threshold for factors such as weather, earthquakes, hurricanes, controlled entry, accessibility, or human threat, a good website takes into account and plans for possible threats.

Setting the stage for a winning website includes making decisions from choosing among hosting options, open source or custom CMS for your website platform, site back-up, Flash vs. non-Flash (are we still having this debate?), in-house or out-source, DIY SEO or professional SEO, third-party verification programs, shopping carts, merchants, and a host of other factors that determine how well your website would survive an event.

What kind of event am I suggesting? Think of Victoria Secret's first online fashion show that took down the entire platform, or the hack into Amazon.com that took the website down and resulted in lost revenue. Some events are preventable, some will not be, which is why it is imperative you be prepared.

Some Unexpected Events Are GOOD!

Not every event is negative. We all hope for that day when our content, video, or blog post goes viral because of media coverage, endorsement, or unsolicited promotion. Unfortunately, when your website crashes because of the load, it might as well be a missile fired by from your competitor to take your website down (another very good reason to never host your website on premises). You must consider these events and plan for them when planning your website. It could happen—and often does when you least expect it. Prepare for the worst and hope for the best. After all, who creates a website hoping to remain anonymous?

Data Is Worth Its Weight in Gold

Protect your data and relationships. You must create a plan that enables you to recreate the website in minutes or hours (depending on size), should something happen to the infrastructure of your website.

This can be achieved through a balance of well-timed back-ups. Whether you choose to back-up to the cloud, to your own hardware, or a combination thereof; it is imperative you back-up the website, data and related owned assets, including those which reside on third-party platforms. We will touch on this in subsequent chapters.

Planning for Production

Once you have completed the Website Planning phase, defined website architecture and requirements, you will want to include all vital processes in the implementation of the mission, and strategy.

The following is an outline of what the Website Production Process might look like:

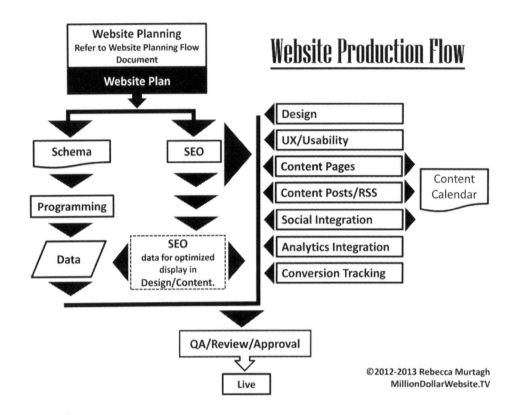

Website Production Flow

Website Planning
Refer to Website Planning Flow Document

Website Plan

Schema

SEO

Programming

Data

SEO
data for optimized display in Design/Content.

Design

UX/Usability

Content Pages

Content Posts/RSS

Social Integration

Analytics Integration

Conversion Tracking

Content Calendar

QA/Review/Approval

Live

©2012-2013 Rebecca Murtagh
MillionDollarWebsite.TV

Chapter 16:

Make it Mobile

The discussion of mobile deliberately precedes the Website Design chapter. Here's why:

The World Is Mobile

In 2012 Internet users will access the web with more mobile devices than desktops. Mobile device adoption is expected to increase exponentially in the next few years. So much so that Intel has begun to reflect a decline in PC sales in projections to shareholders.

The use of mobile devices such as Smartphones, the iPad, Nexus, Kindle, Nook, and other tablet devices is on the rise by consumers and professionals. How consumers use mobile is changing the way websites are consumed. Every organization should expect a percentage of website visitors to be using mobile devices.

Many organizations have never considered what the mobile experience is for their visitors. Have you viewed your website on multiple mobile platforms to see what visitors see? Chances are you can do more for your mobile customers. This is especially true for websites built with Adobe Flash because Apple iOS devices (and now Google Android devices) will not support Flash.

Mobile Search

One of the most frequent tasks users perform with a mobile device is search. Searches conducted from mobile devices result in conversion at a higher rate than from other devices, and conversion often occurs shortly after a mobile search (Keynote Systems, Inc., 2012).

As of July 2012, Google enjoyed a 94 percent share of US mobile searches.

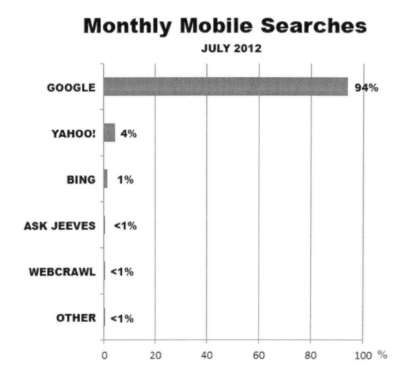

Google Crawls and Indexes Mobile Sites Differently

How search-friendly your mobile site is and how it relates to your primary website and domain directly impacts your overall performance in search, so it is wise to include mobile in website design, content, usability, and conversion planning.

Google is fully invested in the mobile space. In fact, in December 2011, Google launched Googlebot Mobile to crawl and index the web the way a Smartphone does. Because Google dominates search, it is imperative that you consider the following guidelines offered by Google on its Webmaster Blog in June 2012:

Google supports three different mobile website configurations.

1. Sites that use responsive web design (RWD) deliver the website to all devices on the same set of URLs, using the same HTML for all devices and relying upon CSS (Cascading Style Sheets) to control how the page is rendered on each device. Responsive web design is not only my recommendation; it is Google's recommended configuration.

2. Sites that dynamically serve all devices on the same set of URLs, but each URL serves different HTML (and CSS) depending on whether the user agent is a desktop or a mobile device.

3. Sites that have separate mobile and desktop sites.

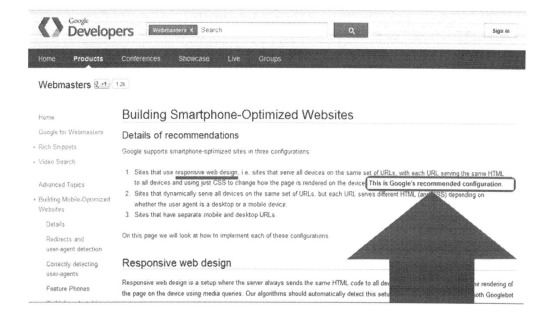

Learn more about Google's position on mobile by visiting links on the website to this and other resources.

Once you've decided not to become obsolete and make the website mobile-friendly, the next question is, how?

There are currently two schools of thought when it comes to mobile websites. I was recently on a mobile website panel where each of us presented slightly different views on which direction was best, when any one of them would work fine in the right hands.

Because either of the two types of websites that serve mobile users will work, it is important you have some key information before deciding which is best for your organization.

Single Website or Separate Websites?

In keeping Google's recommendations in mind, there are two schools of thought when it comes to creating the ultimate mobile experience: building one site or creating separate website for mobile.

Choice 1: Single Website for all users

One of the most efficient and effective ways to seamlessly serve website visitors across all devices is by building one website using responsive web design. This is my preference and what I recommend to clients who care about search, economy of scale, and website management over time. As I mentioned previously, Google also recommends it, which is why MillionDollarWebsite.TV , the website for this book, features a responsive design.

Responsive Web Design

Responsive web design is perhaps the cleanest, most cost-efficient approach because the website is coded to automatically adapt website display to the device the website visitor is using. The beauty of responsive web design is that you create the website once and do not have the added expense of creating and managing multiple versions that must be continually updated as new mobile devices come on the marketplace. The responsive website makes updates seamless because all versions reside on one website, eliminating the concern of being punished by search engines for duplicate content if not managed properly. In addition, it streamlines the website management process, which is when the rubber really hits the road. With only one website to manage, costs can be managed.

In addition to being identified as the preferred method to go mobile by Google, responsive design is considered a best practice and should not cost more than traditional design. If someone tries to tell you that it does, move on to the next vendor if you are outsourcing. However, when comparing "traditional" website design and responsive design, you now know that the latter will serve your needs better, so a slightly greater cost on the front end could save you a great deal of money later. If you wish to have a responsive website, you must include this in your RFP or website site requirements to avoid additional cost or schedule delays later. I recently watched a client's project come to a halt when, despite my recommendation to include it in website requirements and the final contract, they waited until final website designs were presented to inform the vendor that they wished to have a responsive website built. Understandably, the web firm brought the discussion back to budget, timeline, and project scope because responsive design was not even on this firm's radar and they had never built a website this way.

If your web design resources are in-house, you would be well served to provide tools and training for responsive web design. If you are a small business or do-it-yourselfer, responsive design is readily available in WordPress and Drupal themes sold online by several reputable providers and is built into low-cost website design programs, like the one we used to create MillionDollarWebsite.TV. I provide links to responsive theme providers as well as a link for a free trial to one of the most affordable WYSIWYG theme generators on the website for you to explore. Responsive design should not be cost prohibitive.

Choice 2: Stand-alone Mobile Site.

Not to be confused with a mobile app, which would be independent of the website strategy, the independent mobile website is a separate entity from the primary website and resides on a separate domain. As such, they are crawled and indexed separately, and duplication of content can be a detriment if not managed properly by an experienced website developer.

The two-site approach is often the result of a decision influenced by the desire to meet very specific needs of mobile users, or a really great sales pitch by a mobile website company or vendor. A word of caution here: If there was a compelling reason to include information, features, and conversion mechanisms on your primary website, they merit serious consideration for inclusion in the mobile website as mobile device users have come to expect as much from their mobile experience as they do from the desktop, which has forced many to scale up their mobile experiences to match the website they created for desktop users. So, streamlining the website for a mobile version could prove to be an exercise in futility, fail to deliver conversion, or both.

The independent mobile website requires a separate budget, site plan, design, content, calls to action, and independent maintenance.

No Mobile?

If you have a website that does not fall under either of these categories, you may still have a mobile accessible website. Often a website that was built without mobile as a consideration is not fully functional on mobile devices. If you are faced with living with an existing website for the time being that is not fully functional on mobile, be sure to include core conversion mechanisms from your home page, like a contact phone number or access to a contact form.

Keep in mind, your non-mobile site may not meet the criteria search engines seek for optimum performance and may fall short of serving the increasing volume of your customers who will use mobile devices to research, compare, and complete the purchase decision.

Now that we have addressed the choices you have in meeting the expectations of your mobile customers, let's move on to web design.

Chapter 17:

Website Design

It is important that you read the chapters on Website Strategy, Mission, Architecture, SEO, and Mobile before you read this chapter.

After reading these chapters, it should make perfect sense why the web elite never begin the planning of a new website with design. The result of the work you have done up to this point will greatly enhance the design process. Without proper planning, you are destined to go through many rounds of designs and revisions. Remember, the designer cannot read your mind. When you enter the design discussion prepared, everyone wins.

When to Begin Design Discussion

Because most web vendors "live" in the creative world, or the programming world, it is only natural that their approach to the project begins with that frame of reference. These professionals are not prepared to do the heavy lifting required to enter the design discussion.

I have been privileged to work alongside some of the most talented designers, architects, programmers, and scripters in the industry. Each is trained to solve problems according to their discipline. Their career is measured by their execution of those principles, despite the influence of other factors. Many will collaborate, yet they share the same starting point—solving a problem with their talent. They cannot begin solving the problem until you have identified the problem. They expect you to have done this work to plan the website before they begin breathing life into it. I have guided you to have prepared the website strategy, site map, and requirements first, so you will be prepared to discuss design.

Web Design Does Not = A Website

By now you realize that website design is not the website in its entirety. There is much more to creating a user-friendly interface to engage visitors (your customers). The outer shell of the user experience, or graphical user interface (GUI), should be consistent with the brand; reflect website strategy, mission, and architecture (schema and/or site map); perform in search; resonate with target audiences; and promote clicks to conversion. This is a tall order.

You may wonder, what would happen if you ignored my advice and began the website process with design? This is no mystery—it doesn't end well. My colleagues and I have witnessed the outcome of this choice far too often. We are later called to help clients "save them from themselves" when they did not receive the website they expected and needed to be successful.

An astounding number of websites are built on assumptions. You may recall this discussion from earlier chapters. Your strategy and requirements must lead this process.

Lack of Preparation Will Cost You, One Way or Another

When designers do not receive clear direction, they expect that multiple designs, revisions, and redesigns will be needed to get to approval. Some may pad their price to allow for ample design work. Many will include one to two designs in their quote, knowing full well that because the direction provided was not specific enough in articulating requirements, additional design will be required, automatically increasing billable time and the design budget.

Start from Scratch

No matter what you believe, most website designs are not created from scratch. Designers often purchase templates, themes, or put a slightly new spin on previous designs. They consider this custom design, making their job easier and increasing their profit margin. Who knows? One of these designs may suit you just fine, but having a designer create a fresh look for your website would be much more desirable. However, approving a less-than-ground-breaking design can still be effective, as long as it effectively meets your requirements, conveys your brand, delivers value to visitors, and promotes conversion.

The Cart before the Horse

For argument's sake, let's say you couldn't resist. Because of cost, time, or simply falling in love with a website design, your website is suddenly being led by the confines of a cool, hip design or a downloaded template. How bad could it be? After all, the creator has built dozens, hundreds, or thousands of websites that appear to be doing just fine.

Just because a designer's end products look good does not mean they deliver results. And, one step further, many website owners have no idea whether their website is fulfilling its potential and serving the bottom line. So, remain objective when reviewing a website portfolio, and remember that you can engage one resource for design and another to build it out.

Facing the Inevitable

Let's say you ignored my advice and went with that generic website that does not specifically address the needs of your customers, business, or brand. It is inevitable that you will make changes soon, and often, until you adapt to meet the demands of your customers.

Growth Ready

When you do not approach the website using methods of the web elite (strategy, mission, site map), it is likely that you will need to invest more time and effort later to accommodate growth. Your website can grow with you, at least for some length of time, when you have taken the time to properly plan and articulate the needs of your organization. The framework I provide you throughout this book will help you create a framework that will enable you to accommodate change and growth without reinventing the wheel or starting from scratch.

Web Design Basics

There are many creative influences on website design, so there is no way I can squeeze everything you need to know about website design into this book. And, you do not have to be a designer to appreciate good website design.

So, in this chapter I want to focus on the fundamentals you can use to have productive conversations with your designer, to guide the design discussion with clients if you are the designer, and to evaluate templates and themes if you decide to go it alone.

The digital space has evolved quite a bit over the years and will continue to change. I have outlined web design best practices to enable you to evaluate your website design options.

The Home Page

You have approximately two to three seconds to capture your visitors' attention, no matter what page they land on. As the front door of your website, the home page must achieve the following:

- Let visitors know they have come to the right place.

- Convey brand.

- Include data for search engines.

- Engage visitors.

- Promote clicks to pages or other calls to action.

Failing to earn that click typically results in that visitor abandoning the page which negatively impacts key performance metrics. When a visitor leaves quickly, "time on site" is reduced; when a visitor leaves without clicking on any other page, a "bounce" results, which also counts against Google's ranking of your website in SRPs (search engine results pages).

The following are methods the web elite deploy to win the click:

Designing for the Web

- Use web-safe colors. Using the "hex color palette" enables your design to be interpreted across multiple browsers more consistently than colors used in print.

- Do not attempt to use print design, such as brochures, to drive web design decisions; they serve entirely different purposes and require unique approaches.

- Consider user experiences across all devices (desktop, mobile, tablet, gaming devices, etc.) when planning functionality, navigation, image, and content. Deploying one responsive web design enables your primary website to be mobile friendly without having to invest in a separate website and Google recommends it.

- Review design layouts from an SEO perspective before the design is applied to code. Look for compliance with best practices in search engine crawl-ability, page load time, "above-the-fold" data, navigation, etc. Be sure to include content on each and every page, beginning with the home page.

- Create an attractive design that will appeal to your ideal customers (refer to personas).

- Usability alone will determine the success of a design. Unless the website design serves the user, it has failed.

- Be consistent with your brand.

- Balance your home page to appeal to left-brain as well as right-brain people, balancing graphical and textual messaging to appeal to both users.

- Display access to "mission critical" content through visible navigation above the fold.

- Use heat-map or eye-tracking studies to place the most relevant and important elements where visitors will find them.

- Less is more. White space and simplicity can enhance usability.

- All "controls" (navigation, enrollment, instructions, etc.) must be available at all times to enable users to manage their experience.

Once you have approved a home page design, you will need to define whether all pages will use the same design, or whether a different interface will be applied to second- and third-level pages.

Every Page Is a "Home" Page

Every page is a potential landing page. Visitors will not always enter your website by way of the home page. They could arrive on any page of the website as a result of search, email link, social media share, or referral.

Design (and Content, which we will address in a later chapter) directly impacts the ability of the website pages to appear in search engine results, which can greatly enhance visibility to target audiences. When content is organized and optimized to serve the customer in all three phases of the purchase decision, conversion is more likely. We address this further in the chapter on SEO. But for planning purposes, because a visitor may bypass your home page completely, the presentation of secondary and tertiary pages is equally important.

Pages

The permanent, static pages of your website are different from posts, which we explore further in the chapter on Content. Access to the most important pages should always be available in website navigation, and the website design should reflect the presentation of pages as indicated in the site map. Planning the website structure upfront makes it easy to add new pages over time. Search engines see and display qualified landing pages in search engine results.

Flashing Is Not Cool

This (along with the move to HTML5 which enables 74 percent of the market to view video) makes Flash a highly risky investment. Because Flash has been used to display video-like visuals (which have historically made usability, accessibility, and SEO next to impossible for web and mobile browsers), we need to look to more globally accepted languages and applications to display content. We will talk about video later, but for now the important takeaway is that because Flash support is disappearing, so will Flash.

Design Is More than Visual

Good website design integrates a number of factors that impact the quality of a user experience. In addition to brand, visual appeal, and usability, performance is high on the list of requirements of Internet users—your customers.

Time Is (NOT) on Your Side

Time is precious. You must reward website visitors for visiting your website. If you do not provide the information, solution, or answer they are seeking in a timely fashion, they will move on to the next website, most likely that of your competitor(s). And, statistics show that they will not return. This is a fatal blow you want to avoid after all you have invested to earn that click.

Consider the following:

- 47 percent of consumers expect a web page to load in two seconds or less.

- 40 percent of people abandon a website that takes more than three seconds to load.

- A one-second delay in page response can result in a 7 percent reduction in conversions.

- If an e-commerce site is making $100,000 per day, a one-second page delay would cost approximately $2.5 million in lost sales every year.

- 79 percent of dissatisfied shoppers are less likely to buy from an online site again. (KISSmetrics, 2012)

Design and SEO

The website elite know from experience how much website design matters to SEO. Ask the web elite to evaluate SEO of a website, and the first thing they will likely do is "View Source." Why? Because the source code displays what search engines "see."

Search engines do not view your website the way humans do. Instead, search engines view the data that creates the website that humans see. (Remember what we discussed in the SEO chapter: The Google Knowledge Graph seeks data. Your data is what is left after you distill away the code created by the platform, CMS, applications, and programming elements used to display the graphical user interface.)

Viewing the source code of your website reveals key information that search engines algorithms use to calculate search engine rank, such as:

- Data / Information

- Text (Data) to Code Ratio

- Assets (graphics, video, etc.)

- Links

Reading source code effectively does require some level of understanding of HTML. However, anyone can see source code of any website through their browser.

How to View Source Code

Want to see your website the way search engines do? You can view source code on your home page or any page or post on your website. (Each will be different.) Each Internet browser and version will display access to source code slightly differently. The following samples will give you an idea of what to look for.

View Source in Firefox

In Firefox, you can right-click on the background or main area of your website which will pop up a menu from which you can select "View Source."

View Source Code in IE – Internet Explorer

Internet Explorer also offers access to source code via right-click.

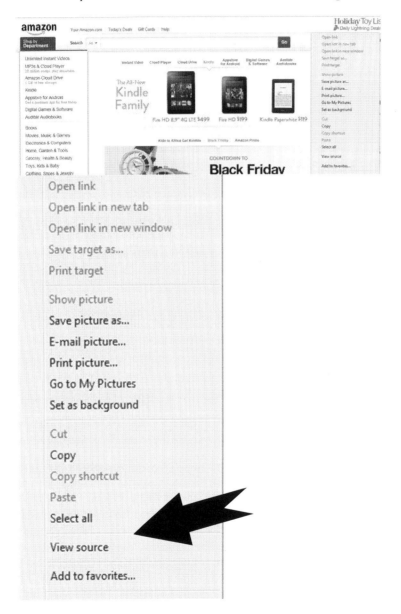

Source Code Is Merely a Reflection

Unlike the actual code used to create the website, the source code is a mere reflection of how each page and post has been created. It can be viewed by anyone but cannot be modified by public visitors.

To the experienced eye, the source code of any website page or post will reveal:

- Level of SEO – whether or not the website has been optimized for search

- White Hat vs. Black Hat SEO – Source will quickly reveal whether a website has been optimized in a way that could put it at risk for blacklisting or delisting.

- Proper formatting of content for visibility

- Which keywords the website uses to optimize

- Which third-party programs the website integrates (email, CRM, plug-ins, Google tools, etc.)

- Placement of important data in the proper places on each page

- Compliance with "Quality" website guidelines set forth by the World Wide Web Consortium and search engines

W3C and You

W3C (World Wide Web Consortium) has established standards for the building and rendering of website pages, including HTML, CSS, SVG, device APIs, and other technologies for web applications that are recognized worldwide as the authority when creating websites. The entire w3.org website is dedicated to promoting best practices for HTML, CSS, Javascript, PNG, Webfonts, and a host of related topics that those who design and build websites can reference.

You do not have to master these methods in order to lead the creation of a successful website. However, you can control your own awareness of these methods. And, you can require the website that will represent your brand or business be compliant. In that spirit, although most web professionals do build according to W3C standards, you may want to specify it as a requirement to those who will design and program the website.

You can learn more about Website Design and Applications, Standards, the Semantic Web and much more from the W3C website: www.w3.org/standards/

Prioritizing SEO in Design

Unfortunately most website designers do not appreciate the reality that what they create will impact the performance of the website. It is incumbent upon the brand or business to do the work I've outlined in preparing strategy and SEO before entering into the design discussion.

Use Data to Drive Design Discussion

Whether you are building a brand-new website or redesigning an existing website, your website strategy and mission will guide you toward making good, solid decisions in website design.

The user experience should be a primary driving force of website design. Designing the website without considering the perspective of the audience the website is designed to serve could create a major disconnect between intention and reality.

Data generated by users on the existing website will enable you to conduct a fairly thorough study of how visitors consumed the content and features within the design of the old website. This should include analysis of the home page, as well as landing pages, to identify user behavior that can be leveraged in planning for a new website design or theme.

In Page Analytics

One of the easiest tools to access is Google 'In Page Analytics'. Many people do not even realize they have access to this invaluable insight right from their Google Analytics account. In Page Analytics appears under Content in the newest version of GA and can be used on any page of your website. It will display what percentage of clicks on each page went to each navigation button, link, graphic, or post and tells you what percentage of clicks are "below the fold." Most of your clicks should be above the fold. To make use of this data, review where visitors click most, and if they are not finding navigation, calls to action, or content links that support your goals, you will want to revisit format, placement, and presentation. If your visitors prefer graphics, use them more often. If they prefer text links, be sure to make your content clickable.

The following is a sample of analytics from my personal blog home page.

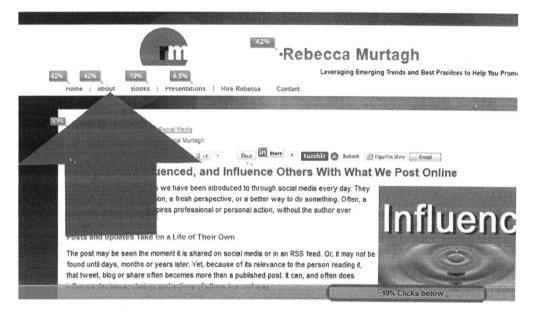

As you can see, Google Analytics displays exactly where visitors click.

Above the Fold

The "fold" is considered to be everything that appears in the web browser when a page loads. In light of the wide variation in OS, browser, and resolution settings used by visitors, it is imperative that you present mission-critical content above the fold. Search engines Google, Yahoo!, and Bing consider presenting key content above the fold part of a "quality website."

Note the orange bar on the Google Analytics image identifies 18 percent of clicks on this page as occurring below "the fold," which means 82 percent of clicks are above the fold. This is an important consideration that many, many designers overlook. It is not on their radar because they design the page as a whole, rather than considering how it will load on devices that will view the site.

What you include above the fold is important. Having too many advertisements above the fold is discouraged for SEO purposes. In January 2012 Google began penalizing for having too many ads, which not only impacts what displays "above the fold," but it can also slow the page load, for a trifecta of demerits related to search.

Users do not want to have to scroll down the page to find the content that drew them to the page in the first place. A balance between content, images, navigation, calls to action, and ads achieves the best results, so be sure to give this some thought when planning or reviewing website design.

Mission Critical Design Elements:

- Primary Navigation

- Home Button/Icon

- Conversion Call to Action

- Primary messaging or Initial Content

Google Analytics 'In Page Analytics' are extremely helpful, but you may be looking for additional, more in-depth insight about user experiences on your website to guide your decisions moving forward.

Can You Take the Heat?

… heat-map studies that is. Heat maps interpret user behavior on your website to visually represent the concentration of clicks. Google Analytics 'In Page Analytics' offers a visual representation of where the most attention and activity occurs.

Eye Tracking

Eye-tracking studies act similarly to heat-map studies, except they track the movement of the human eye, rather than clicks. Eye tracking is popular offline as well and is typically used by consumer brands and retailers to test packaging and placement for product in various settings.

The Design Grid

One of the methods used to plan website content is the design grid. Using a graph-like grid to map out the foundation of the website graphical user interface (GUI) can go a long way in planning the user experience before getting into the actual design phase. This simple step can save considerable time and expense in web-design services.

Tips for using the design grid to plan website design:

- Use the site map as your guide.

- Identify the "fold" and plan accordingly.

- Designate navigation placement.

- Plan content areas (text, RSS feeds, video, social media, etc.).

- Determine where ads will be placed.

- Reserve space for the footer.

If you are presented with a choice between a static page width and length or dynamic dimensions depending on browser and page content, the grid will enable you to ensure you offer a quality experience for users that search engines will likely approve.

Google offers a graphical representation, which can be interpreted as a grid, displaying how visible the website will be to visitors, based on the device used.

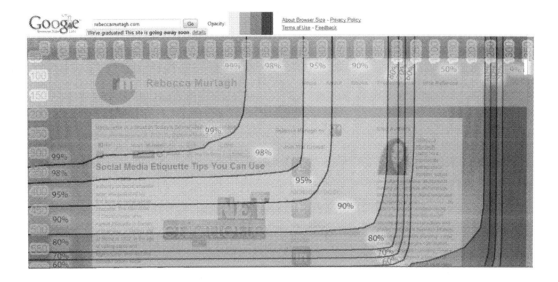

Website Design Basics

The following are some basic guidelines I use to communicate with my clients' design vendors that you may also find useful.

Designing for All 3 Phases of the Purchase Decision

The three phases of the purchase decision create different expectations from visitors. The website design should include considerations of each customer type at any one of the three phases of the purchase decision.

When planning and reviewing website pages and posts, consider the following:

- Does the design make it easy for visitors to find the information they seek in making an informed decision?

- Is access to all relative information easily accessible?

- Are unique selling points and competitive differences clear?

- Are calls to action clear?

- Does the website make it easy for visitors to engage with the brand?

- Always include access to the home page.

- Make the most important (and popular) navigation, features, and content visible and clickable from the top left corner of the website (where most eyes begin their view of web content).

- Balance graphics and text. This not only promotes appeal to natural preferences of both left-brain and right-brain users, it also promotes usability and search engine friendliness.

- When possible, present at least one set of links to primary, mission-critical pages as text navigation, somewhere on the website.

- Resist hover or "catch me if you can" navigation and focus on what makes the user experience as easy as possible so they focus on the message instead of trying to find their way around the website.

- Offer at least one conversion mechanism on every page and post. You never know if it is a visitor's first, third, or 10th visit to your website.

- Proactively present offers, buttons, icons, graphics, or links that promote conversion throughout the website.

- Use web-safe colors when building a website to ensure accurate and consistent presentation across all browsers and devices. Refer to a Hex Color Chart when planning and approving a color scheme that is consistent with your brand for website design.

Always include a footer. The footer is a good place to offer navigation to important pages that did not fit or make the cut for primary navigation but should still be accessible from all pages. Or, to feature mission-critical content. Users know to look at the footer if they do not see what they are looking for, so the footer can be a valuable complement to site-wide navigation. Resist the temptation to bulk up the footer with keywords for SEO purposes as Matt Cutts, head of the Web Spam team of Google, has indicated that Google has "done a good job" of ignoring boilerplate, "site-wide links."

So, currently, these links may not be weighted. However, they have been in the past and promote usability and access to pages that do not fit in navigation important to visitors.

Here's an example of how the footer could complement primary navigation if primary navigation were to include:

Home

Products

Services

About

Contact

A complementary footer might include:

Home

Products

Services

Our History

Support

Map and Directions

Promotions

Note the addition of promotions on the footer vs. primary navigation. This is intentional to allow traffic resulting from email, direct mail, mobile marketing, or social media to land on the actual page which can be tracked in analytics. However, some visitors will want to return to the page at a later date, so it may make sense to include it on the footer.

- Include copyright, year, and the name of the entity that owns the website. Date should span the first date of oldest content up to the current year.

- PLEASE update copyright date every year! Nothing makes a website look stale and old faster than an outdated copyright (which is visible to Google as well, by the way).

- Never, never, never include a link to the website designer, developer, or any other third party at the bottom of your home page or site-wide footer. Google takes a very strong position on linking, and the last thing you need to do from your home page is diminish the authority of your website. If you are required to include a link to another website from your home page, be sure to direct it to open in a new browser window, otherwise you are sending away the visitors you have worked so hard to get to your website. You would be shocked by how many websites fail to implement this simple step that sends visitors away. If the link is to a website with more authority than your own, within your "sphere of influence" it may not hurt you. This could be a parent company, overseeing entity, strategic partnership, etc. Unless you are in the Internet business, it does you no good to link to your web designer, developer, or SEO firm. Not to mention, if they are associated with entities that are considered to be in "bad neighborhoods," that could also transfer back to you.

- Links *to* your website are as important as links *from* your website. Google has become very discriminating about link relationships and will penalize your website if too many links from those "bad neighborhoods" lead to your website. You can identify referral links to your website by using tools like Open Site Explorer, which will let you check three domains free per day; you can upgrade to pro to manage more than three or to access various other site management and SEO tools.

- It is preferred that you link only to websites with more authority than your own. If you must include links to other websites and you are unsure whether they are in a good "neighborhood," designate links to other websites as "no-follow," which suggests to search engines that you do not want them to transfer your authority to the destination URL. This is merely a suggestion, but it can be useful if you are concerned you are giving away your search engine "juice" or confusing Google about who you are when they connect the dots between your website and relationships.

- Avoid dated functions like blinking text and huge hyperlinks—they date your website. I know, this should be common sense, but I was shocked recently when visiting a reputable company's website that featured flashing text. What were they thinking? Just remember, to today's savvy Internet users, this kind of retro is just not cool.

- Resist the temptation to trade design for function. Navigating your website should not be a mystery. You have only two to three seconds before visitors make their next click. Hiding navigation or key functions could prompt a visitor to make that next click "back" to the search engine or competitor's website.

- Text is your friend. Do not present all your copy as graphics or part of a Flash movie. Delivering your content this way is not only invisible to search engines, it can also be difficult or impossible for visitors to increase type size with keyboard commands, or to have text-to-voice readers convey brand messaging.

- The Favicon: These little icons appear in browser windows and tabs when your website loads. These tiny little graphics offer a little bit of real estate on the user experience that can and should be used to promote your brand. Because the square is tiny, you want to keep it simple, but your website should include one. There are many quick ways to create the .ico graphic required to load in browsers, depending on how your website experience is being built. Your designer/developer can add the graphic in a snap. This 5- to 10-minute exercise will go a long way to elevate the visibility of your brand. If you are building your own website, you can find tools online that will convert .png or graphic files to the .ico format required. Various WordPress plug-ins and themes will place the favicon in the proper place for you if you are not code savvy. The most important takeaway is to keep it simple so that the graphic is identifiable.

Chapter 18:

Content and Copy

Content is King…Yesterday, Today, and Always!

I have been an advocate for content-rich websites since the early days—long before it was cool and became such a hot topic. In recent years, many have jumped on the bandwagon, stressing the importance of content, but few master the rules the way the web elite do.

Content = Data

If you read the chapter on SEO, you know that the substance of your website (Content and Copy) create the data that search engines use to present you to your customers.

One of the most common mistakes in writing for the website is repurposing content created for other mediums. The website is a unique animal. It is not a brochure (or shouldn't be). It is not a whitepaper, a legal brief, print catalog, technical manual, or book. The website is an interactive experience that requires action from the individual consuming what you present. So, you had better make sure you understand what your visitors require from you in order to become a customer.

"We don't read pages—we scan them."
– Steve Krug, author of *Don't Make Me Think*.

This is so true. Website visitors rarely read entire pages or posts. They scan them, which makes the formatting of copy and content for effortless consumption as important as the words themselves.

You must communicate enough to make the page worth visiting, but not so much that the visitors are so overwhelmed when they arrive on the page that they miss key points or calls to action.

Content vs. Copy: What's the Difference?

There are exceptions to every rule. However, the following is an example of what Content and Copy might look like for a website.

Copy should make it easy for visitors to understand your value proposition and differentiate you from your competition, and it should promote conversion. Copy typically resides on dominant, permanent pages and plays a specific role in supporting measurable goals. Some might even call this Sales Copy.

Examples of Copy, typically presented in the form of a page:

- About Us Page

- Services Page

- Solutions Page

- Catalog of Products

- Pricing Page

- Plans Page

- Media Room

- Competitive Advantage Page

- Guarantee Page

Content can be defined as the communication you provide to tell your story, without directly asking for the sale. This may include information on the website that tells the story of your brand, provides assistance or value to customers, shares opinion and/or insight, and subliminally supports your USP (unique selling proposition). Content can be used to educate, persuade, and earn truest. Content might include whitepapers, blog posts, worksheets, editorials, reviews, etc.

Sample Content, typically presented in the form of a post, is:

- How the Latest Technology Affects You

- 4 Reasons You Need Solutions like Ours

- Press Releases

- Product Reviews

- Compare 3 Top [insert product here] Solutions

- Testimonials

- Top 10 Reasons to Invest in [insert solution here]

- How [insert solution here] Impacts the Bottom Line

- When Is the Best Time to Buy [insert solution here]

You get the idea.

KISS – You've Heard It a Million Times ... Keep It Simple Sweetie

Simplicity is worth its weight in gold when it comes to presenting content online. Simplicity does not mean boring, flat, or worthless. Simple can be extremely powerful when planned and executed strategically. Design plays an important role in presenting your content, so be sure to include your creative team in content planning.

Content with a Plan

The web elite know how valuable words are to the quality of a website. As the lifeblood of the website, copy and content should be created within the context of the website strategy and site map. Once the website has gone live, the Content Calendar is what keeps the website fresh and interesting. We expand on the Content Calendar in the Maintenance chapter.

Reward Visitors

Getting a qualified, new visitor to the website is no small feat. You have invested a great deal to earn the right to win that visitor over. Yet, you have only seconds to offer compelling reasons for that visitor to continue consuming your content, or better yet, accept your invitation to become a customer.

Hold Nothing Back

So often, especially in the technology sector, clients tell me that they could never reveal their unique value proposition on the website because it would provide too much insight to their competitors.

News Flash: If your solution is good, your competitors are likely already aware of it, may have access to it, and are actively benchmarking against it. Trying to keep your solution a secret, even if you are first to market, hurts you more than your competitors. After all, once they have successfully met, or exceeded, the threshold you have created and shared it with the market, they become the leader, rather than the follower.

Protect Your Secret Sauce

I am in no way suggesting you reveal your "secret sauce," proprietary or intellectual property that enables you to solve the problem, whether you have created the most incredible chocolate cupcake recipe in the world, an invention that solves an everyday problem in an exciting new way, or complex software that can cut operating costs of companies by 50 percent. What I am suggesting is that you thoroughly explain how you solve the problem, highlighting why your solution is superior to others.

In addition to making it extremely easy for visitors to find the content they need to make an informed decision, your website is in the very unique position to make a compelling case for your brand. The website has a private audience with the visitor for as long as they decide to stay. Only you can reveal what makes your brand the best, and doing so is the best way to enable visitors to prequalify and convert themselves to a lead or customer.

If you wish to protect your "secret sauce," require users to register with a valid email address in order to gain access to specific content, link, access to download a document, or access to a demo or sample. Keep in mind, if your prospects have no idea what is behind the curtain, they will have no incentive to explore further. Internet users are much more protective of their email addresses and will not submit them freely unless they believe they are receiving something of value and are serious about initiating a relationship with your brand.

Location, Location, Location

Geo-location is important to every website at some level. Without localization, your website essentially competes against every website in the world, especially in search. Over the years, I have seen far too many website designers, agencies, and programmers omit even basic location data from websites.

Without location information, a service provider, retail store, hotel, restaurant, spa, transportation, community organization, or any number of businesses are at a distinct disadvantage when competing for new business. Because search engines often display results in the geographic proximity of the individual conducting the search by using the IP address, location is an important item to include in planning Content and SEO.

Exercise: Refer to the Website Worksheet to define your target geographic market and be sure to optimize the website accordingly.

Automate, Automate, Automate

One of the most attractive benefits of conducting business online is that you can make money while you sleep. Of course I'm simplifying this a bit, yet regardless of your business model, you can conduct business at all hours of the day or night, without having to be "present." I'm not suggesting you let your website go live and run on autopilot indefinitely. What I do advocate is using quality content, calls to action, and mechanisms to let customers advance along the path from visitor to customer, no matter what day of the week or hour of the day or night they happen upon your website.

If you truly want to generate leads, build your list, sell your product, book your services, collect donations, or whatever your mission involves, you must automate as many processes as possible, like completing a form; entering an email address; booking an appointment; purchasing products, services, or time; enrolling; registering; uploading information; or any number of functions that make the visit worthwhile for visitors.

Moment of Truth

The moment of truth for any website is whether it can trigger a decision (conversion). Google calls this the "Zero Moment of Truth", or ZMOT. They stress this so much that Google's Vice President of US Sales and Service Jim Lecinski wrote a book on it. You can download the eBook *Zero Moment of Truth* for free.

You can't add just any content and be rewarded. However, strategically increasing your relevance to the way your audiences seek and consume information as it relates to your offer (product, service, idea, brand, etc.) will elevate the visibility of your brand to customers in every phase of the purchase cycle to transform visitors into customers.

The Rules of Website Content Are Simple

- Make every page worthy of the time visitors will have to invest to consume it.

- Write original content, without exception.

- Follow your Site Map and Content Calendar to maintain the integrity of website architecture, SEO, and conversion paths for each customer persona.

- Always post digital content to your website first whenever possible. This is especially true when content is syndicated or distributed by others in context of news, press releases, announcements, etc. Search engines credit only the first to publish and may penalize your website in search if your content is published on another website or domain before you post it on your own website.

- Offer breadcrumbs that put visitors in control of the user experience with text links to important pages and resources within the narrative on pages.

- Direct all offers to your website, offering unique content, even if some version is available on another platform (Facebook, LinkedIn, Twitter, email, etc.).

- Do not build entire campaigns on a platform owned by someone else with their own agenda. Always bring them home (to your website) so that you can tell the whole story, link to other assets on the website, follow up with customized emails, extend offers, invite engagement, measure performance, and proactively manage the relationship you have worked so hard to earn.

Get Fresh!

I have been preaching to clients for years about the value in continually updating their websites—not just because visitors want to know you are active and engaged with the world around you, but because search engines also value a relevant website. In November 2011 Google launched the "Freshness Update," preceded by the Caffeine Update specifically to crawl the web to find fresh content.

Takeaway? Because Google believes that those searching want results that are "relevant and fresh," the fresher you keep your website content, the more likely Google is to find it.

Creating the Win-Win

Think about your website now. What are your customers looking for? How will they use your product or service? How can you become a more integral part of that process? How can you entice them to return for additional products or services over time? What value can you bring to their life (personal or professional)? When you put the needs of your customers ahead of your goals, the entire user experience takes on a new life.

For example, the website Zappos.com is far more than an online shoe store. Zappos has created an online shopping experience where the relationship with the customer is the primary product. Zappos has become a powerful benchmark for the user-centric shopping experience.

Other examples of customer-centric shopping experiences include LandsEnd.com, Amazon.com, and TripAdvisor.com. Each has become a market leader in their space by anticipating the needs of their customers and responding with conveniences that differentiate them from their competitors.

Exercise:
Think about what your website could offer that would make your website unique you're your competitors. Is there a service or convenience feature that you could offer that would promote loyalty to your brand online?

Winning Hearts and Minds

Consumers have many places to shop online. And, yes, I am speaking B2B (business to business) as well as B2C (business to consumer). Whether you are in the business of serving businesses or consumers, the best way to attract and win customers is to offer an online experience that honors the customer. Forget about implementing the most innovative technology or design. If your primary online strategy is not built around meeting the needs your customers, your brand will not fulfill its potential online.

It is imperative that you throw away any preconceived notions about what you want to see on your website and adapt that thinking to what your customers would like to experience on your website. Once you embrace the power of the website visitor, you immediately jump far ahead of 70–80 percent (possibly even more) of all websites who view the website merely as a place to broadcast information about their brand.

Set Your Sight on Goals

Notice I say "Goals" not "Goal." Building a new website is not the goal. "We need a new website" is often the dialogue that initiates a stream of discussions about what it will look like, who will build it, and what the budget will be before the most important questions are even asked. I know—I've witnessed it firsthand for 16 years. Only after a website is built, bought, and paid for and then fails to deliver a return on investment, do many determine something is wrong and seek out more experienced people like myself to right the ship, so to speak. This is unfortunate, and it doesn't have to be this way.

A *Million Dollar Website* achieves multiple goals by design:

- Clicks to Conversion

- Visibility and Accessibility

- Design and Usability

- Content and Sharing

- Features and Function

We walk through each of these goals as building blocks to be used in developing your business strategy. I do not use technical industry jargon, but plain language to enable you to identify the goals that will drive your online strategy. Organizing your goals according to this format helps you create a balanced approach to creating a *Million Dollar Website*, on any budget.

IMPORTANT! Do NOT skip this vital process. If you don't know what you want to achieve, how can you possibly begin the process to get there? You wouldn't build a house without blueprints, or travel a long distance without a map, guide, or GPS, would you? Consider this your road map, your blueprint for success. Once you have addressed the five goals, you have the information needed to develop a deliberate plan for your website. You can use this plan to communicate your vision with your team, to guide the creation of your own website, or to use as a framework for an RFP that is more likely to enable you to receive more accurate proposals and true apples-to-apples comparison when selecting vendor(s).

Opportunity Lies Ahead

Whether you go through the goal process alone, with a team, consult colleagues, or tap into the expertise of a seasoned pro, it is this part of the process from which ideas for truly powerful sites come to be.

And, although I would love to tell you that your website plan should be concrete and never change, the truth is every once in a while, somewhere in the process you or one of your team will have an epiphany, an idea that could take the website from good to great. If you have done this work in establishing your goals, you will have the framework to determine quickly whether any new content, feature, application, or program will support your website mission.

Heart and Soul

The website is a window to the heart and soul of the brand. Just as the store window is designed to entice you to take that all-important step to walk inside a store, the website must entice the click.

Click to what? What should be featured on your website? What you feature on the website home or landing page is part of the strategic planning process. Good design will always provoke a reaction. On the web, the primary objective is to get them to click to another page on your website.

What's in a Click?

A "click" is defined by how many times a website page is loaded. A "visit," however, is defined by how many sessions have visited your website. A "unique visitor" further defines how many unique people have visited your website. These terms are often confused by website owners, executives, and marketers, so it is important that you understand the difference. This is also a very important factor in analyzing website performance through analytics, which I don't have ample room to cover properly in this book, but which I do cover in much greater detail in Google Analytics and Strategy seminars and webinars.

Getting a visitor to your website is the first goal. Whether achieved by search, advertising, social media, QR bar code, or mobile app, the primary goal is achieved when your target audience accepts your invitation to visit your website. What they do when they arrive is equally important.

Failure to entice a website visitor to click on another page results in a bounce, and a bounce represents more than a missed opportunity to sell your brand, product, service, or idea. Most bounces occur because the page the visitor landed on did not deliver on the promise your visitor expected when they accepted the invitation to visit. A bounce also contributes to the website's Bounce Rate, which is among many factors used by search engines to determine the quality of results. When your website qualifies to appear high in search results for a specific keyword or phrase, and a high percentage of clicks from that search engine result in a bounce to and from your website, it can negatively impact your performance in search over time.

Chapter 19:

Public Relations and Media Relations

Public Relations has evolved tremendously over recent years. According to a survey conducted in 2007 by the Arketi Group, 100 percent of journalists surveyed stated they rely on the Internet to help get their job done.

Journalists invest around 20 hours a week developing story ideas on the Internet. Because they could be located in any time zone or location, providing public relations and media kits online has become highly effective in facilitating media coverage.

When asked how they use the Internet, journalists responded:

- 98 percent say reading news

- 97 percent say emailing

- 93 percent say finding news sources

- 89 percent say finding story ideas

- 72 percent say reading blogs

- 67 percent say watching webinars or webcasts (Allen)

How Do Journalists Find Sources?

Because journalists rely upon the Internet for story ideas and to research stories they write, it is important to note that 85 percent of journalists say companies without a website are less credible.

One study of print and online journalists revealed that Google is most visited for research. Wikipedia is second. Of those surveyed, 89 percent said they look to blogs for story research, 65 percent go to social networking sites such as Facebook and LinkedIn, and 52 percent look to Twitter and other social platforms (Cision, 2010).

Bottom line: If you are not using your website, social media, and search to publish search engine-friendly news, your brand could elude today's Internet-savvy journalist.

President and CEO of The Buyer Group and writer at SearchEngineWatch.com, Lisa Buyer explains it well;

"Public relations really reside on your company website or your blog. Unlike the past, press releases, press kits, images, social networks, fact sheets should all be headquartered on your website within a public relations online newsroom.

The online newsroom provides a way to deliver news 24/7, not just for journalists, but also for visitors of your website."

Journalists view the following pieces of information as most useful on a corporate website:

- contact information – 97 percent

- search capabilities – 95 percent

- press room/press kits – 92 percent

- company backgrounders – 89 percent

- publication-quality graphics or photos – 66 percent (Allen)

Press Releases

RSS feeds are ideal for press releases. They enable interested readers to subscribe to the feed to receive posts automatically, which can greatly enhance readability. Because RSS adoption remains low, you may also consider implementing an RSS-to-email application to enable people to receive notification of posts as they are published via email. An additional benefit to RSS is that search engines crawl RSS content differently and can be notified essentially in real time when new content is posted. This is exactly why you want your RSS content (blog, press releases, news feed, etc.) to reside on your primary domain.

Buyer offered this additional insight on the value of an online press room:

"When a journalist is writing a story at 3 in the morning, they don't have to look for that press release; they just go to your website. They should be able to go to your news section and look up bios of senior management, information about the event they may be looking to write about, images and video to be able to put together what they need to know for that story."

So, if you wish to attract media coverage for your next new invention, latest software, innovative service, or book, invest the time and energy in social media. Connect with clients, customers, vendors, and yes, even your competitors.

Media Relations

You don't always get a second chance to tell your story. Missing that all-important call or media request could greatly diminish or eliminate the media coverage you are seeking.

To facilitate further engagement you will want to provide access to appropriate contacts for journalists, editors, fact-checkers, researchers, etc. Be sure to follow PR guidelines that include contact information. If you do not wish to display personal emails or phone numbers publicly, you may consider adding directing media inquiries to a unique contact form for the Press Room or Contact Form that will result in delivery of a media request to an email account that is monitored by one or more persons to provide responses 24/7 365 days per year.

Chapter 20:

Social Media

By now you realize that no website lives alone. Authority is greatly influenced by the relationship between social media and websites.

Social media can be intimidating and difficult to quantify for some. While some brands see social media as a vital extension of their brand, others view social media as a frivolous concept unworthy of their brand. Most struggle to justify social media from a cost and benefit perspective until they understand how it influences users and can enhance perceived authority by search engines.

Before you decide how to approach social media and its relationship to your website, I invite you to read on to understand what the web elite understand to be true about how social media impacts brands in every imaginable industry, and why it is part of the high-performance website.

Facebook Is Not Your Friend

In fact, social media platforms should never be considered a legitimate replacement for having your very own website.

The web elite know better than to hand over relationships with customers to Facebook or any other platform.

Sure, Google+, Facebook, LinkedIn, Twitter, Manta, YouTube, Pinterest, and other social media destinations offer a place for you to park your brand and interact with target audiences. And yes, doing so may even attract more interaction than your website. So, go ahead and connect with, engage, and educate your audiences and promote your product and services, but never complete the conversion on someone else's platform. A tremendous amount of data is collected by Facebook and other platforms, however, precious little is transferred to brands and advertisers. This data, as well as a direct relationship with the customer is an asset that should be coveted and protected.

Many organizations seek out help from social media companies to build up the brand's social presence. However, many do not have the whole picture. Because others may not appreciate the value of a customer, or its impact on the bottom line; Never, never, never hand over control of the relationship with target audiences and customers to another entity, unless they are highly experienced and fully understand all aspects of the social landscape.

Social Platforms Are Businesses Too

Each social media platform has been created to generate a profit and support its own goals and objectives, and their objectives have little to do with the success of your brand, even if it seems as though they want to be of value. Whether they are aggregating users to sell advertising (like Facebook does) or data to authenticate people and develop artificial intelligence that drives technology (like Google does), or selling memberships to facilitate specific interactions for the purposes of employment and networking (like LinkedIn does), the bottom line for them is to achieve their goals, not yours. And, what happens when that platform takes a left turn that flies in the face of your brand, goes under, or is sold to an entity that competes with your brand? You must be in control of your destiny.

"Social Media and Search" is a topic I often speak about at industry conferences and corporate training sessions. The connection between these two platforms evolves so quickly, it can be difficult to keep up. How you choose to approach social media directly impacts the performance of your brands competing online.

If you take nothing else away on this topic, please remember this:

Social media and search are vital to the website that intends to compete for and win new customers online. If you wish to compete and win in the digital landscape, you must be prepared to engage with individual customers wherever they are.

I know, some of you are murmuring to yourselves that your industry doesn't belong on social media or that your customers are not on social media. To that I say hogwash.

Your customers are online.

If you represent a B2B company, you are sure to find your clients, vendors, and competitors online—with or without participation from your brand.

Got Media?

Remember that newspapers, magazines, trade publications, television, and radio rely very heavily on social media for stories. If they view social media as a "real-time" reflection of what is going on in the business landscape you operate in, wouldn't it be a good idea for you to be there as well?

You know the saying: "Keep your friends close and your enemies even closer."

Social media is also an extremely efficient way to monitor your industry and what the media is covering, to keep tabs on competitors, and with a little luck, you may even get that next great idea from a tweet, a post, or a conversation.

3 Simple Rules of Social

There are three simple rules the web elite understand about the relationship between the website and social media.

1. Social media is a marketing channel for promoting your brand, visibility and engagement.

2. The website should always be ultimate destination for engagement.

3. Social Media is a vital ingredient to SEO and as such requires strategic planning and execution.

The web elite know from experience how important social media is to the website and they take it seriously. The "shoot from the hip" approach to assign a resource with some extra time to manage social media without a strategic plan and intent is not only a waste of time and energy, but it can do more harm than good.

Over the last few years I have observed organizations of all sizes and industries cast their line into social media only to fail, determining that social media offers no value to their organization. Failing to realize results is usually a direct result of random acts of interaction that offered no value to the brand or to the audiences it would aspire to engage on social media.

Social media platforms are free. However, despite what they may promote, they are not in the business of helping you build your business. The more traffic and time spent on the platform, the more ad revenue and data they can generate—good for them, not so good for you.

It is imperative that you approach social media as strategically as you approached the website or any other marketing or sales initiative.

Exercise: Adapt your website strategy and mission to create a social media strategy and mission.

One Size Does Not Fit All

Social media strategy should be unique to each brand and its customers. What works for one organization does not always translate to others, so be sure to give some thought before setting out to make your mark on the social scene. And, for goodness sake, please do not assume that the neighbor's nephew in his third year of college is the best candidate to manage your social media (or your website for that matter!). These assets reflect your business and brand and require as much thought and management as you invest in marketing, business operations, sales, and customer service. In fact, if you are smart about it, the website and social media can be used to improve the efficiency and effectiveness of a variety of day-to-day business functions.

Home Sweet Home

Remember, social media is "earned media" that holds value to the *Million Dollar Website*. One of the most common mistakes brands make when deploying social media is to leave their audience on the social media platform, or even worse, they direct engagement from the website to the social platform without a deliberate path to return. An example of this is building a Facebook store and getting so caught up in the ego aspect of this feat that you forget that you no longer control the relationship on Facebook—you lose valuable data and direct access to your customers. If you want to reward Facebook followers, or friends, fans, or connections of any other social platform with an offer specific to them, go for it. But be sure to maintain a diligent "listening campaign" to respond to questions, complaints, or reviews related to your brand. Otherwise, consider using social media as a marketing channel to bring them home to your brand's website.

Remember, the website should be the ultimate destination for social audiences.

7 Reasons to Bring 'Em Home

The following are benefits to leveraging your website as the primary destination from social media:

1. It's YOUR customer. Bringing social audiences to your website enables you to nurture, measure, manage, and sustain the relationship over time.

2. Data. You can only glean insights that will help you serve your customers better if you are able to collect, analyze, and act on data generated from user experiences, promotions, and offers on your website—exactly why social platforms want to keep your customers on their platform.

3. The "referral" created when your social audiences click from the social platform to your website via your profile or an update can help your website's visibility in search.

4. Brand. A moment in time on a social platform can't possibly tell your brand's story. The social click to your website creates an opportunity to expand their exposure to your brand story and win a customer for life.

5. Conversion. When your social audience responds to an offer and is directed to your website, you have more control over the conversion. You can create specific landing pages, conduct A/B testing, customize, upsell or cross-sell, collect data, follow-up with auto-responders, and more.

6. Quality. You can respond to the needs of your customers and continually improve your offering when you take ownership of the relationship with your customers. Leaving your customer on a social platform like Facebook makes your customer Facebook's customer first.

7. Support. It is far easier to support your customers when you are in command of the environment they are using. Recently a client told me they had to create a dedicated email address just to answer customer service requests made in the Facebook timeline. Ideally, a customer request would receive a personal response on Facebook for all to see, but then that customer would be extended an invitation to access existing customer service channels (phone, warranty registration, contact form, support ticket, whatever this may mean to the individual business).

Always, Always, Always bring the relationship back to your website. The website is an environment you can use to cultivate meaningful relationship with customers.

Social Media Is More than Socializing

If you still think social media is a waste of time or not a valid marketing channel for your brand, I highly encourage you to follow me on Twitter (@VirtualMarketer), on LinkedIn, or on Google+ where I share the latest in emerging trends, including opinions of other thought-leaders from across the web. It does not matter if your website is about a consumer brand, start-up, one product, a service business, book, or your own personal blog. Social media is a landscape you and your customers share, and it is a powerful influence on day-to-day personal and business decisions.

Social Has Power

When you visit a new city and are looking for a good restaurant, chances are very good you will perform a search on Google or some other platform. Just as you—as a private citizen—interact with and are influenced by friends online, so will your customers be. It is imperative that you implement some level of monitoring or reputation management program. You want to be among the first to see comments made about your brand online.

Search engines have begun to integrate various rating and review systems into organic search results. Google used to post their own reviews until in 2012 when they moved to integrate Zagat reviews. Bing integrates Yelp reviews. The bottom line is, even if the players change, customers care about reviews, so search engines care about reviews. And, in case you think that it doesn't matter what they say as long as they are talking about your brand, you should know engine algorithms are now smart enough to discern between positive and negative feedback, impacting search results accordingly.

Still Not Convinced?

Let me share an example of how powerful social media can be on your brand and website. Recently I stayed at a hotel while on a business trip. It was an absolutely horrendous experience. After requesting to speak to a manager at the front desk, I was told there was none on duty. I was provided a business card with a manager's name and phone number. A few hours after I checked out, I left a voice mail requesting a call back to discuss the hotel experience. No reply. A few days later, another of my unanswered calls went to voice mail, so I left another message emphasizing the request for a call back to share an unpleasant guest experience. I never received a call back— that is until after I posted a review on one of the review sites. Within hours, I received a call from the manager apologizing for the delayed response, citing that corporate headquarters for this hotel brand had contacted him after reading my review. Now if that is not validation for monitoring your brand on social media, I don't know what is.

Ratings with Benefits

Social media also influences search engine visibility. Search engine algorithms are keen on determining authority by connecting the dots between reviews, customer sentiment, and your brand. The more prolific your reviewers are, the more visible your website becomes.

There is obviously more to the relationship between reviews and website visibility than I can get into in the context of creating the website. My objective is to elevate your awareness and appreciation for your customers' power. If you are very good at what you do, you may want to link to review sites from your website. I recently saw a small contractor website do this quite effectively. He understood how important reviews are to his customers, so he linked to the reviews posted about his business on ServiceMaster. There are numerous destinations for your clients and customers to gain insight from other customers depending on what type of business you are in. Become familiar with them, frequently visit them, and respond to complaints, requests, and even positive reviews as promptly as possible to gain full benefit from this "earned media."

Keep Your Ear to the Ground

The last thing you want is to have negative ratings out there. They are seen by your customers and calculated by search engines. It is imperative that you monitor the web for reviews, mentions, and comments. This is called Reputation Management and is a vital aspect of protecting all the good work you will do to build your high-performance website.

You can start monitoring your brand with Google Alerts, but chances are you may want or need greater coverage and data. There are numerous tools available to help you stay on top of social interaction about your brand. The solutions vary depending on the type and size of your business from tools like Radian6 as part of Sales Force, Raven Tools, Sprout, Trackur, Hubspot, and a host of others. I've provided links to various resources on the website MillionDollarWebsite.TV for your access.

Serious Business

How will the next visitor become your next customer, investor, employee, blog writer, friend, fan, follower, affiliate, reseller, or strategic partner? You must invite them!

In the chapter on Conversion, we explore the need to invite conversion on every page of the website in greater detail. In the context of social, integration with the website with items such as social media "share" buttons, links to review pages, third-party review sites or other resources that influence your customers is important.

ROI of Social Media

Calculating the ROI of Social Media and how it directly impacts the performance of the website has eluded marketers for some time. Recently, Google Analytics added *Social Media Reports* to enable reporting and calculation of ROI, making it easier than ever to measure social media traffic, influence of the website on social platforms, and impact on the bottom line.

You can learn more by reading my January 2013 Search Engine Watch guest post; *5 Steps to Calculate Social Media ROI Using Google Analytics.*

.

Chapter 21:

___

Accessibility and Usability

Accessibility is not discussed nearly enough. It should be a natural part of the website process. It does require thought and deliberate consideration, but the benefits make it well worth the investment.

Kristine Schachinger, founder of SiteWithoutWalls.com, Search Engine Watch contributor and an expert in SEO, social media, accessibility, site design, mobile, HTML5, and usability says it well:

"Many companies think of accessibility as the red-headed stepchild of the website consideration process. However, what site owners often fail to realize is the value creating a site that meets accessibility standards offers users and site owners.

When meeting the WCAG AA accessibility standard which is the one used internationally (and unofficially by many US government agencies) you create a site that has clean, light code and a user friendly design. A site that because of the standard is not device dependent, so it is mobile phone capable and feature phone abled. And a site that is future proofed & readied for quick shifts in the development process that can rapidly adapt to market shifts and/or business needs.

Finally, the accessibility market is a trillion dollar untapped market that consists not only of those we typically think of as differently abled, but simply those people getting a tad older (baby boomers), or who are color blind (common), or who simply have dexterity or vision issues.

Oh and if you need one more reason above usability, conversion optimization, lower site maintenance costs and opening new markets? Well, search engines love it."

Usability = User Friendly

By the time your website goes live, you will have invested countless hours and resources to invite new visitors to get to know your brand and hopefully progress from a website visitor to a loyal brand customer. The last thing you want to do is make them work hard to do what you are hoping they will do.

What is usability, you ask? Usability is the website visitor's ability to master their interaction with the digital environment you offer with as little work or effort as possible. Most people view usability as an intangible when, in fact, usability is among the most tangible metrics by which to measure the effectiveness of a website.

One of the best books about website usability is *Don't Make Me Think* by Steve Krug. The title sums it up perfectly. You do not want your website visitors to have to think about what you offer and where to go next. They should be able to easily navigate the website and find and consume content required to determine their path of engagement with your website and brand. The book is a great read for those seeking insight into best practices for usability.

Forget about What You Want

Too many organizations begin planning a new website by creating a "wish list" that reflects their needs rather than creating a quality user experience for customers.

The primary focus of the website should be the user experience for each customer type. Refer to the personas you created to deliver what these customers seek. Then map out each customer type's decision process and what they need to know or have to make their decision. Once you have defined these paths, you can plan how to present that content and promote conversion.

Seconds Count

Most brands pay little attention to details like page-load time until the site begins to slip in search engine results, bounce rate escalates, and conversions decline. Website visitors do not want to wait for any page of a website page to load. In the web industry this is referred to as site speed, latency, or load time.

It will be easier and more cost effective to build a high-performing website from the start, rather than to try to dismantle and correct it later. Understanding how design, data, database integration, software, content, and assets impact site delivery speed and user satisfaction enables you to make more informed decisions.

Having a beautiful website is of no value if your intended audience never sees it. You may be surprised to know how demanding your customers really are.

Website visitors have little patience:

- Two-thirds (64 percent) of mobile and Smartphone users expect a website to load in four seconds or less.

- 60 percent of tablet users expect a site to download in three seconds or less.

- 57 percent of people surveyed expect a bank website to load in two seconds or less.

- Any website in any industry can expect to be held to these standards. Because consumers have high expectations when visiting a website, so do search engines.

Search Engines include site speed in determining search rank.

- In April 2010 Google announced that they were "including a new signal in search ranking algorithms: site speed" to help determine page ranks for terms being searched.

- Yahoo! says a 400ms delay causes a 5–9 percent decrease in traffic.

- Still not convinced site speed is mission critical?

- Website speed can, and will, directly impact your bottom line.

- According to Google, a 500ms delay will result in a 20 percent decrease in website traffic.

- In 2008 Amazon found that 100ms of latency resulted in a 1 percent loss in overall revenue. (Hoff, 2009)

Let's do some math to illustrate how significant that can be. With total sales of $100 billion, 1 percent is $100 million sales lost. You don't have to be making billions or even millions for your bottom line to take a hit due to site speed. Losing 1 percent of any business is significant when it comes to the Internet.

If your business will close only 100 customers in a year at $10,000 per client, that 1 percent equals $10,000 in lost revenue. Or, if you lose 1 percent of your membership, which drives traffic that produces $500,000 in advertising revenue, you have lost $5,000. Gets your attention, doesn't it?

No matter how you slice it, it is business lost. I've seen this firsthand with many clients over the years. They chose graphically intensive websites that were not optimized for speed. As a result, load time was extremely high, as was the bounce rate. After all, visitors can't click a second page if they have given up on loading the initial page. Improving page-load time directly reduces bounce rate and increases page views.

Right about now you may be wondering how long it takes your website to load. Is your website performing within acceptable parameters? Are you losing visitors, or are a high number of visitors abandoning slow-loading pages that result in a higher bounce rate?

There are a few ways to determine site speed. Whoever will be in charge of monitoring and maintaining the website should make reviewing the following on a regular basis (at least once a month). Below are some basic, free tools you can use to stay on top of website speed.

- Google Analytics now include page load times.

- Google Webmaster Tools displays site speed to visitors.

- Yahoo offers a hit-list of 34 rules that affect web page performance for webmasters.

Exercise: Find out whether your website is loading fast enough. Google Webmaster Tools offers this information from a search perspective, and Google Analytics provides this insight on a page-by-page basis.

Speed It Up

Correcting a slow site can be quite simple or complex, depending on the level of sophistication of the culprit pages and how accessible the code or administration for the website is. Sometimes it is as simple as replacing a complex script with simple text and links, or breaking a large page up into smaller pages with a planned flow. At other times, reducing latency is much more involved, requiring a deconstruction of a page to a simpler form. Worst-case scenarios require a complete rebuild of the entire website.

There is always a way to reduce page-load time. If you consider page load a priority, be sure to include it in website requirements.

Walk a Mile

One of the best ways to test how successfully your website will serve target audiences is to walk a mile, or click a path in their shoes. Adopt the personality of each customer and create a path for each of the three phases of the purchase decision to insure your website will meet their needs, regardless of where they are in making their decision.

Paths for one persona in each of the three phases of the purchase decision might look like this:

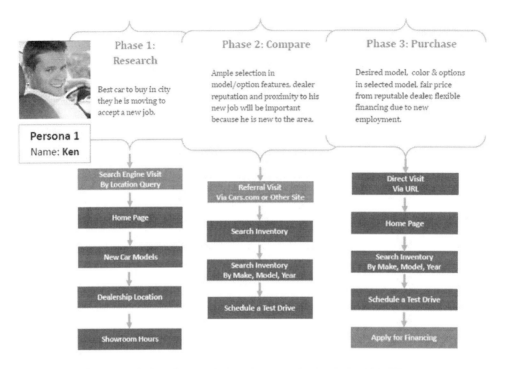

Usability Will Make or Break Your Website

Accessibility is often overlooked and over-sacrificed for the sake of design and function. When the customer gives up on a website because it is too difficult to navigate, doesn't produce quality search results for product or information, takes too long to load, or cannot be viewed by the device they are using, that is a problem that needs to be fixed.

There are some thresholds that dictate what is deemed acceptable when it comes to things that evolve over time, such as browser version. For example, you may not be able to accommodate someone visiting your website using a very old browser version. Dr. Jakob Nielsen, a recognized expert in usability, maintains a website called Alertbox that provides regular updates on topics related to website usability if you wish to stay current on the topic.

What Is Accessibility?

Some define it as accessibility for those with a sight or hearing disability. I prefer to think of it as making your site available to all users of all abilities and disabilities, regardless of how they view, listen to, or access your website. The introduction of the touch screen has significantly impacted usability for websites. Some are easier, some are more difficult to use. And, let's talk Flash for a moment. Aside from tools or special applications, I am not a fan of Flash. As a user, I have always found being forced to sit through a fancy movie-like introduction a waste of time. It turns out most Internet users agree. And, let's also mention that Apple, in its fundamental refusal to integrate use of any Adobe applications, will not display Flash websites. One more consideration is the barrier that Flash creates when optimizing content. If your mission is to compete for and win new business using your website, leave the Flash to advertising agencies, car manufacturers, and other "experience-minded" brands.

There are some great resources that cover accessibility in depth. Let me share some basic guidelines that are easy to follow and will prevent you from having to reinvent the wheel later when you realize that you have excluded some of your audience.

Measuring Usability

Usability can be monitored and measured in a variety of ways. One of the most powerful tools is a heat map generated by tracking eye movement and clicks on each page of the website. This exercise, although extremely insightful, can be cost prohibitive for many organizations. An alternative is to use website data generated by programs such as Google Analytics, Omniture, WebTrends, and other programs. Each will interpret and display data slightly differently. However, they each offer insight into key data, such as:

- How many visitors were there to each specific page or result?

- What elements on the page they clicked on?

- What percentage clicked on those elements?

- How did visitors arrive on key pages?

- What path did visitors take throughout the website?

- What percentage of page visitors responded to calls to action?

- What percentage of visitors were converted to customers?

- How accessible is the brand to visitors and customers?

Does the website promote relationships?

Some refer to the System Usability Scale (SUS) when scoring usability of a website. SUS was created in 1986 to measure usability of computer programs, long before the commercial Internet became saturated with websites. Proper application of this scale eludes many, despite its popularity.

Jeff Sauro, a recognized expert in usability, offers an explanation of the System Usability Scale (SUS) on his website, along with various reports, tools, and resources designed to assist in the quest for a successful website user experience.

Four of the 10 questions used by the SUS process provide the foundation from which to evaluate the usability of the experience your website offers visitors.

They are:

1. This website is easy to use.

2. I am able to find what I need quickly on this website.

3. I enjoy using the website.

4. It is easy to navigate within the website.

These four points are extremely relevant to usability and conversion of the high-performance website. Many web designers have never been exposed to usability standards and do not incorporate usability into their design process, which is exactly why it must be included in requirements and considered throughout the process.

Exercise:

Once you have defined paths for your customers, take a moment to assess the existing website using these four points and use this process to identify opportunities to improve.

Chapter 22:

Be Sticky

Okay, you've done all the good work to plan the website. Now it is the moment of truth … can you keep a visitor on your website long enough to make them a customer?

So many good things in life are sticky—watermelon, cotton candy, sticky buns, barbeque ribs, etc. Websites are no different—in fact, the stickier the better.

Your Website Should Be Super Sticky

The good news: it takes only two to three seconds for a visitor to determine whether they will go beyond the first page they visit on the website.

The bad news: it takes only two to three seconds for a visitor to determine whether they will go beyond the first page they visit on the website.

Avoid the Bounce

A bounce is the measurement of a website visit that ends with the very first page visited. This can be the home page or any other page on the website. Bounces are bad for several reasons:

- A bounce means you've not only lost the website visitor, but you've lost a potential customer.

- Bounces elevate the "Bounce Rate," one of hundreds of factors search engines take into account when determining search rank and visibility.

- Bounces reduce the average "Time on Site" statistic, impacting search and conversion.

The benefits of keeping visitors on the website longer:

- Visitors become more acquainted with brand, products, services, etc.

- Visitors have a better chance of finding something to like—or love—about your offer.

- There is a higher likelihood visitors will share your website content, news, and offers with others.

- Visitors become more qualified with every page they click.

- Customers become more loyal to the brand.

- There is an increased potential for conversion and ROI.

Be Captivating

Depending on your brand, this can be done in a multitude of ways. "Captivating" will mean different things for each brand and its customers.

Some brands will turn to comedy to win the hearts and minds of website visitors; others will turn to education, entertainment, socialization, or a culture of personal interaction. Whichever you choose, you must remain consistent with your brand. The better you know your audiences, the easier these decisions are. If you are unsure, perform a test by creating a test page that only recipients of a special invitation via email or social media link will gain access to. Closely monitor behavior and response.

Chapter 23:

The Golden Rule

As the ultimate destination for your brand, the website is often the first and sometimes the only vehicle by which you have opportunity to win new customers and build a relationship with each and every customer.

One to One

Your website has done its job when a customer embraces your brand, purchases your product, adopts your method, enrolls in your program, becomes a member, registers for an event, or crosses the threshold with one of any other conversions. From that moment on, you have the opportunity to create a relationship with that individual. This connection should not only be coveted and promoted, but also respected.

Treat Your Customers as You Would Like to Be Treated

That first interaction with your brand gives you permission to communicate with that customer and earn their continued loyalty and business. Unfortunately, many get overly zealous in taking advantage of this connection and turn their customers off. Try to resist the temptation to inundate your new customer with communication, sales offers, promotions, or news. Instead, offer customers the ability to select what type of communication they are interested in receiving from you (managed easily by any good email program), and always provide the ability for them to unsubscribe to your communications. It's good manners, and it's the law.

Because the website is a business asset and is an active extension of your organization, it is important you are aware of this and other legal implications that relate to the website.

Chapter 24:

Your Website and the Law

In the early days, the Internet was compared to the Wild, Wild West because there were next to no rules, industry standards, or laws to govern the digital landscape. It was only a matter of time, though, before regulations came to be, and there are legal implications that you should be aware of and include in the decisions you make when building a website.

CAN SPAM ACT

The CAN SPAM ACT, which is United States law, sets forth rules and requirements for commercial email communication. This needs to be part of the website discussion because you can, and should be, inviting visitors to opt in to email lists, submit quote requests or contact you via a form, and/or provide an email address and other data when completing a conversion on your website (membership, purchase, enrollment, donation, registration, etc.).

You would be surprised how many agencies and design and marketing firms are unfamiliar with these laws, and at the end of the day, you are responsible for communications generated from your website or organization.

I highly recommend you visit the link to the page created by the United States government to become familiar with these legal guidelines.

Privacy Policy

Every website should have a privacy policy. This is another aspect of the website often overlooked even by seemingly experienced web vendors. The privacy policy is extremely important to your organization. Whether you are simply collecting email addresses, phone numbers, personal or business data, serving up recommendations based on previous purchases, or sending promotional emails to customers after they have made a purchase, it is imperative that you define and place a privacy policy on your website.

The FTC (Federal Trade Commission) enforces how companies collect, use, and secure consumers' personal information. So, you will want to make sure your organization follows the privacy policy by implementing reasonable security measures to protect your customer data. The FTC stresses on their website that failure to follow your business' own privacy policy can result in costly legal fees. The Small Business Administration (SBA) offers an overview of privacy laws and resources to assist in implementing a privacy policy for your organization.

Copyright

No discussion about the website would be complete without a discussion about copyrights.

The website is a public media platform. As such, the publisher (your organization) is responsible for what you put on the website.

When faced with creating a website, catalog, community, blog, or directory, it is imperative that you understand copyright and ownership of content. When you create a unique body of work (such as pages, posts, images, and video), you inherently own the copyright.

In August 2012, the *Wall Street Journal* reported that Google will begin to penalize websites suspected of improperly posting copyrighted material. Translation: your website will perform poorly in search. Maybe not today, maybe not tomorrow, but you can expect that once Google has posted such a position, they can, and will, fully enforce it, as they always do.

To establish the copyright for your assets, you will want to include the © copyright symbol accompanied by the entity that owns the content on the home page of your website. Be sure to include the current year in your copyright notice, even if you have not made any changes, and update it each and every year. Failure to do so indicates to visitors (and search engines) that the site is old and outdated. If you want, you could include a copyright date back to the earliest date of content creation.

So, your copyright notice could look like either of the following examples:

©2013 Your Company Name
©2009-2013 Your Company Name

Duplicate Content Is a Big Fat NO!

There is never really a good reason for duplicating content owned by another entity on your website, even if you have legal permission to do so, as part of a licensing, distribution, or resale relationship.

Here's why:

- Copyrighted assets are unique and owned by the creator. This applies to you and others. You would not want your competitor to use the content, images, video, and graphics you created to promote their business. The same is true when it comes to copyrights of others.

- Duplication of content is not only discouraged, but punished by search engines. This is touched upon in the chapter on Content from a search perspective. From a legal perspective, duplication of content is risky and can cost you, especially when the owner has taken the time to register online assets with the government.

- If you want your brand to stand out, common content should only be the beginning. When you are prepared to customize data, product, and other feeds specifically for your website, the payoff is usually significant.

Having said this, I do realize there are exceptions to every rule and that there are real-life scenarios that may require a delicate negotiation or balance between unique and duplicate content. I have witnessed this firsthand with a consumer-brand client that creates celebrity-branded product. Despite repeated efforts, one of these high-profile designer brands has insisted that the brief, standard language they provide (and was used elsewhere) be used without modification to a single character. Needless to say, this was not the ideal scenario, but we did our best to make it work.

As with any other business decision, you will need to make a variety of decisions that will not be clear cut or black and white. Hopefully the information I provide you in this book enables you to feel more informed and empowered to face such decisions.

Registering Copyright for Your Online Works

Adding the © notice to your website is typically enough to notify others of your ownership of assets on the website. However, if you expect others to be tempted to duplicate your digital property, you can register online works with the US Copyright Office. This includes websites, home pages, and content delivered over FTP. The link above provides a detailed description of how the copyright works and includes application information.

Trademark

Trademarks come into play in very specific aspects of the website. The first is the domain. As the Internet address for your website, the implications of the domain are huge—from a branding perspective and from a search engine perspective. If you are thinking about registering a domain that conveniently reads or sounds like your competitors or like a licensed trademark, think again.

".com" domains are still available, especially if you have a unique brand (Optum3.TV), product name (Kindle), or if you add a geographic location to the name of your business or your primary reason for "being" (Manhattan Dry Cleaners). You can expect that most brands have secured the domains for trademarks. However, as new domain extensions become available, some are tempted to scoop up domains that cross the line. And, some register domains innocently, not knowing someone owns a trademark that might entitle them to secure the domain after your purchase.

It is always wise to do your homework—search brands on Google and the USPTO (US Patent and Trademark Office) database before registering a unique domain to save yourself the time, money, and stress of a legal battle later.

Chapter 25:

Be Prepared for Success

Creating a *Million Dollar Website* is only half of the proposition. The other half is being prepared to deliver what you are selling. One of the most painful mistakes you can make is to not be prepared for the success you seek.

Sounds crazy? Believe me, not only is it true, but I have witnessed this firsthand, far too many times. Some businesses do everything right. They invest in a digital extension of their business only to lose it all just because they failed to adapt their business to accept the success the website would bring. Some went out of business completely; others regrouped and re-launched. All lost the goodwill they'd earned with customers and damaged their brand for a very long time, if not permanently.

Even if you did everything right, your efforts will have been in vain the moment you fail to deliver the offer your customers have accepted.

Real-World Insight: Artist Turned Entrepreneur

On one of my trips to Hawaii, I came across a line of fantastic Hawaiian shirts. Because I was a graphic designer early in my career, I was impressed by the design and images.

I struck up a conversation with the man selling the shirts and expressed my appreciation for the art. It turns out, he was the business owner. He was also the artist—a Hawaiian, and a tattoo artist, with a talent for creating images reminiscent of ancient Polynesian drawings. These shirts were essentially wearable art and refreshingly unique compared to the gazillion run-of-the-mill touristy T-shirts being sold around Hawaii. I observed his table and racks for some time. He was constantly busy talking with people who enjoyed learning about his art as much as they did purchasing items for sale. His personal story also added value to his brand.

There were only a few graphic designs featured, but they were very good and available on various colors of quality short-sleeve and long-sleeve T-shirts and polo shirts for men, women, and youth. Oh, and did I mention that they were reasonably priced too? Most customers bought more than one shirt. He was doing so much right!

I bought a few shirts for the men in my life, all of whom had been to Hawaii. They absolutely loved them—and believe me, they are very particular.

This entrepreneur created a business around his unique talent. He includes the website URL on each shirt (which features his brand), so of course I visited his website once I returned home. I was surprised and disappointed to see the website featured only a sampling of the shirts I had seen him display on the Islands. In fact, the website didn't even come close to creating the conditions that made his in-person sales experience so compelling. I never placed an online order and never returned to the website again. (Remember earlier I spoke of that "one chance" with customers? This is a perfect example of that.)

On my next trip to Hawaii, just a few months later, I returned to the resort where he displayed and sold his shirts twice a week. I was surprised to see a much smaller selection—very few designs and for men only, in limited sizes and colors, no youth or women's shirts.

I greeted him and told him how pleased my guys were with the shirts. He smiled, thanked me, and quickly asked if I'd been to the website as he pointed to it on one of the shirts. Before I could respond, he explained he'd been forced to take the website down. I asked him why, and he told me he simply could not keep up with the orders. He went on to share how people returning to the resort (as I had) were requesting multiple shirts because his shirts were no longer available online. He described one couple who wanted to buy 10 shirts, but he did not have the correct sizes. He was actively sabotaging the very business he had worked so hard to build from scratch.

As I was commenting what an enviable situation to have, especially in a down economy, he told me he was about to put the website back up again. Our conversation ended at the close of our sale, as he attended to another customer. I walked away knowing that because he had done so much right, this should never have happened. Yet, it does. I wrote this book to try to prevent this from happening to others like this gentleman. Please don't let this happen to you. Be prepared for success, embrace it, run with it, and enjoy it!

There is another excellent example on my personal blog (RebeccaMurtagh.com) outlining how Southwest Airlines took a big hit from website, customer service, and PR failure generated by overwhelming response to a Facebook promotion and how they recovered.

Bottom line, be prepared!

Chapter 26:

Website Budget

Winning Websites Are Worth More,
But Don't Need to Cost More

The amount of money you invest in the website does not correlate directly to your website's quality and performance. Extremely costly websites may not perform, and affordable websites can be highly effective. An ample budget does not guarantee that the website will be error free, meet industry standards, or deliver a return on investment.

Remember the client with the Flash website I mentioned earlier in the book? They invested a sizable budget twice with the very same agency, despite the fact that the website could not be found in the top 20 pages of Google search results. I could provide countless examples of expensive websites failing to deliver results.

The perceived value of a website has gone down in recent years—not just because of the abundance of open platforms, plug-ins, widgets, and apps, but also because the volume of demand for websites is enormous. This is simple economics. As a result, to be competitive, firms providing websites have reduced fees. Unfortunately, this has squeezed the profit margin to be so much smaller than in the past that volume is key to the survival of many companies delivering website services. What does this mean to you? More often than not, there is no correlation between fee structure and quality of website services.

I have witnessed this so many times over the years, it is scary. The same RFP can attract proposals that are extremely different in cost and value. The key to getting the right website at the right price is to proactively manage the process.

Sometimes you will get what you pay for. By this I mean if you choose one of those "free" website programs, you must know that you are trading away something. For example, Website Tonight, a simple website framework offered by Go Daddy limits control over structure and is not extremely friendly to content organization, integrating calls to action, mechanisms need to promote conversion, and SEO. There are other players in this space, such as Web.com that tells you they will build you a website for free and "promote it" on search engines Google, Yahoo!, Bing, etc. for a monthly fee. Despite the perception that this is a search engine optimized website, these are often simple websites built to rely upon PPC (paid advertisements in search), from which the vendor earns a percentage from every dollar invested.

What Should a Website Cost?

There is no definitive answer to this question. I sure wish there was because it would be much easier for organizations to define their budgets and more difficult for vendors to charge fees that do not reflect value and ROI.

When determining your budget, always consider the cost and benefit for each aspect of your website. Your goals will guide the allocation of resources and budget, but where does the actual budget begin? This depends on several factors. If you are in a highly competitive space and introducing a new website, your investment may be greater than if you were enhancing an existing website that has been in existence and had some success over the years.

What you will demand from the website should drive budget allocation. If you expect little performance from the website, you can, and should, be able to get a very professional solution for a reasonable price.

The website budget is not a random number. How much you should invest in your website will be directly impacted by the many decisions I guide you through in this book.

5 Aspects of the Website Budget

There are essentially five costs related to the creation of a website. Each is equally important and should be represented accordingly in the budget.

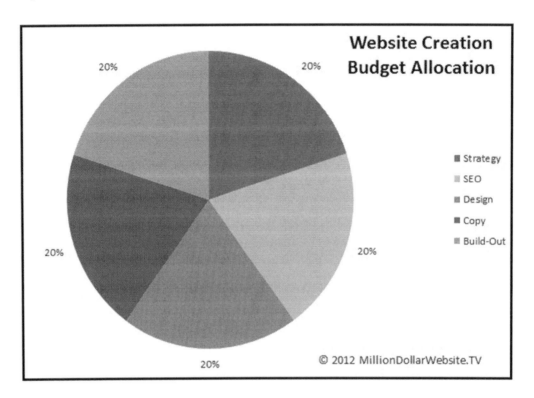

Strategy and Planning

Strategy is imperative to the success of any website, yet few organizations allocate any portion of the budget to it. I recommend 20 percent of the budget be set aside for strategy and planning. As discussed in the chapter on Strategy, this may call for the assistance of a seasoned expert to guide the executive team through the process and articulate the communication required to translate strategy into an actionable website plan.

The cost to engage an e-business or website strategist may vary, depending on how involved they will be in the implementation of the strategy. When engaging an expert to guide you through the strategy and planning process, be sure to articulate responsibilities and whether they will extend to guidance during website creation and review. For best results, seek expertise across all areas of e-business—site usability, SEO, content, etc.—to create a proactive strategy that will deliver results.

SEO

As you know from reading this book, SEO is much more than keywords and metadata. Because of this, I recommend another 20 percent of the budget be allocated for SEO. Search engine performance requires that strategy be translated through optimization at the earliest stages of the website process. Because Google, Yahoo!, and Bing stress the value of a "Quality Website" in search engine rank, SEO extends beyond keywords and metadata to architecture, design, content, page speed, quality of links, and a host of factors.

Do not skimp on SEO if you will rely upon organic search engine traffic to your website in order to achieve any of your goals.

"The first thing I am often asked is, 'How much is SEO going to cost me?'. What you really need to ask is, 'How much will NOT doing SEO cost me",

says Alan K'necht, author of *The Last Original Idea*, Founding partner at Digital Always Media and co-host of #SocialChat on Twitter.

You can achieve your SEO objectives in one of three ways:

1. Hire an experienced in-house SEO. Look for an experienced, respected expert with a minimum of three years' experience.

2. Engage an outside SEO expert consultant to complement or guide your team. Again, seek an experienced, respected expert with a minimum of three years' experience.

3. Train a member of your team to learn SEO. Realistically this person should accumulate two to three years of hands-on experience before attempting to guide comprehensive SEO strategy and implementation.

Design and Usability

Website design does not stand alone. Design and usability are extremely important to the performance of a website and deserve 20 percent of the budget. Website design can be acquired as a standalone service when others are responsible for SEO, content, development, scripting, etc.

Or, you can hire a web design firm to provide the entire website. However, you are not required to hire a design firm to build your website. You could choose to hire a designer to create a custom theme, template, and website design as a flat-file, which developers and scripters can then break down into code. I have been involved in numerous websites built with this approach, which can be an extremely effective approach to executing your strategy. When hiring the designer to build the website, plan additional oversight and review, even if they represent that they include other services. A large number of design firms have added services like SEO, copywriting, etc. to generate revenue without having ample expertise to execute those services.

Try to avoid proprietary CMS (customer management systems) that will lock you into that vendor indefinitely, or customization that alters the inherent benefits of Open Source platforms like WordPress, Drupal, etc. Your website is an asset that you should own, free and clear. You want to ensure you have the ability to preserve the data and assets of the website should you decide to move the website, the relationship is terminated, or the business changes hands or is dissolved at a future date. And, be sure to include social media integration from the beginning of the design process.

Build-Out

Never underestimate the value of the website build-out and allocate another 20 percent of your budget to it. Strategy and optimization are worthless if the website is not created as specified by someone with experience. There are far too many decisions to be made in the construction of a website to leave it to chance or inexperience. The guesswork is minimized when using Open Source platforms, compared to building from HTML or HTML5. Regardless of the platform, execution by an experienced professional will take much less time and will function better than learning as you go.

Copywriting

Because copy is a vital asset of the website and generates the "data" search engines seek to connect websites with customers seeking information and answers in search, you should allocate 20 percent of your budget to copywriting. SEO is a vitally important aspect of website content and copy. Those responsible for SEO should be able to write your copy, or optimize the copy you provide. Refer to the chapter on Copy and Content to define requirements for the internal or external resources that will be responsible for copywriting. Add social sharing mechanisms to the requirements to enable visitors to react to, respond to, and share your content.

ROI

Return on investment is how you will measure success of the website. Whether you are selling product, services, membership, registration, access, information, or are soliciting donations or venture capital, website performance can, and should be measured.

What is a customer worth? Assign a dollar amount to each type of customer. Perhaps a sale = $10,000 in revenue; membership = $100; services = $7,000; investor capital = $1 million; and information = $25. Once you calculate conversion rate from visitors for each type of customer, you can project ROI and measure accordingly. You can also assign dollar amounts to conversions in Google Analytics to connect visitor behavior with the bottom line.

CAC (Cost to Acquire a Customer)

How many website visitors do you need to create enough customers to be successful?

Whether your organizations sells to other organizations, the government, or directly to consumers, you must generate more in revenue than the website costs in order to be profitable. I realize this should be common sense. But, if there is one thing I've learned over the years, it is that common sense isn't always common, especially when it comes to navigating all the hype and salesmanship around website features and services.

Cost and profitability will vary, depending on what methods you deploy to create the website, what portion of the asset will be generated in-house or outsourced, and what the expected return on investment (ROI) is per customer, CAC can be calculated by average sale, revenue generated over the life of a customer, or the influence that customer will have to generate new customers. So, how do you determine the cost of customer acquisition for a website?

How to Calculate Website CAC

Website creation costs include costs to plan, create, and optimize the website to go live. Each is equally important. Success depends upon successful implementation of all to acquire enough new customers to achieve stated goals for less than the cost of the website.

- Strategic Planning

- SEO (including Social Integration)

- Design & Usability (including Social Integration)

- Copywriting

- Build-Out: Custom Development, Programming & Scripting

The following costs related to the performance of the website can be considered part of operational, marketing, and advertising budgets:

- Maintenance

- Digital Advertising (PPC, banner ads, directories, etc.)

- Affiliate Programs

- Email

- Software: Legacy and Third-Party Software Licensing and Integration (CRM, shopping cart, accounting, membership, community, etc.)

- Marketing and PR (including social media, press releases, events, promotion, etc.)

- Training to Build, Optimize and/or Manage the Website

- Maintenance and Management

Digital Advertising

Not every website requires paid advertising or search ads to achieve its goals; therefore, I recommend anything from 0 to 10 percent of your budget be allocated to digital advertising.

Search engine marketing (SEM) is typically deployed in the form of PPC advertising on Google Adwords, Yahoo! Advertising, Facebook ads, etc.

Of clicks in search, 80 percent go to top five organic results; 70 percent are on the top three organic results. This leaves a small percentage of clicks for paid, or sponsored, results. Think about it: how often do you click on search engine "sponsored links"? When I ask that question, nearly everyone tells me "never." If you are not clicking, what makes you think your customers will? Not to mention paid search ads rotate, so you are in a never-ending competition for a position in the rotation and pay more for top slots—PPC and CPM budgets rarely, if ever, go down.

Most people do not click on search engine ads unless they view a special deal or cannot find the result they were seeking in organic search. This is why I emphasize that promotion is the best use for paid search, when it can be proactively integrated with news, specials, discounts, etc. Websites built to depend on PPC are destined to cost more than a website optimized for organic search over time. Be sure to read the chapter on SEO for more insight on how search works for most brands.

Once you have determined the cost to acquire a customer, (which could become your website budget which we will discuss later in the book), you have defined exactly what the website must deliver for you to be profitable. We explore countless methods that can greatly improve the potential that the website will deliver what is required to be profitable.

Alternative Budgeting Methods

Some organizations prefer to allocate a lump sum to the website as it relates to the annual budget.

One of the equations I have used to manage clients' expectations in recent years is that the website is to begin with a working figure equal to 15 percent of the annual revenue the website will be responsible for or will contribute to generating.

If that amount is unknown, you should allocate 25 percent of the marketing budget for the entire year into the website and related assets (social media, photography, videography, etc.). This reflects the contribution of the website to the bottom line. Of course, it also heightens the expectation that it will pay for itself and contribute to the growth of the business.

I know what you are thinking—that's just nuts. I didn't say organizations are willing to invest this. However, if you were to calculate all that will be required to build, optimize, monitor, analyze, and maintain the website at a competitive level, these figures are more accurate than you might initially believe.

Consider this: You are a expecting to generate $100 million dollars in revenue in the next year. It is not unreasonable that the website investment, in its entirety, equal $15 million. This investment might include training, expert consultants, professional design services, custom programming, application development, allocation of time from salaried personnel, investment in assets such as video, ads, photo shoots, email software, legacy software integration, CRM, SEO, hosting, etc. It doesn't sound so crazy now, does it?

The Modest Budget

Not every organization is a proven commodity or able to project revenue. This is especially true for a startup, a brick-and-mortar just entering the digital space, or the organization that is not yet convinced that their organization should even be on the Internet. (I can't believe that any organization needs to be convinced of the need to be online, but there are still plenty!)

So let's do the math for a more modest organization. If your goal is to make $100,000 in the next year, your budget would be closer to $15,000. I know, this sounds like a great deal of money, especially if you are a DIY (do-it-yourself) webmaster. If you calculate paying yourself for time invested in the website, assisted by a consultant or two, some training, and perhaps the purchase of equipment or services that enable you to fulfill your website mission, a 15 percent investment is quite reasonable.

The Website Is Not an Expense—It Is an Investment

One of the greatest misrepresentations of the website is that it is an expense. It is not. The website is an investment. Or, at least it will be when you can compete online to reach new customers and leverage what you now know to deliver value to your customers. Just as you invest in people, software, and tools, the website enables your organization to generate revenue at a profit. How the website is planned and implemented will directly impact how well the website delivers a return on your investment.

Chapter 27:

The Website Team

Will you build the website in-house, or will you outsource it? This very important decision should be made only after you have defined website strategy, personas, requirements, and the site map.

Organizations of all sizes approach the website with a hybrid approach, combining the expertise of specialists and in-house professionals.

You must resist the temptation to hand off the website. There is so much more to be gained when you own and drive the strategy, even when others will be responsible for building the website. Your involvement throughout the process will improve communication, reviews, approvals, and the post-live analysis of website performance.

Not All Web Resources Are Created Equal

I know this will sound very pessimistic and perhaps even a little cynical: please, please, please understand that just because someone creates websites for a living does not mean that they know what they are doing, or that they are good at it.

There are plenty of outstanding web professionals and vendors dedicated to delivering quality services. Many will do just that. Some will deliver much less than they know. It is incumbent upon you to vet the team that will transform your strategy into a fully functioning website.

Regardless of who will be responsible for building the website, you must not hand over the digital destiny of your business or brand without qualifying the vendor properly. Web designers, programmers, and advertising agencies are not good at connecting the dots between what they will build and how it will impact your bottom line. It is not their job. It is your job.

Do not make role assignments based on what you expect your team or vendors to know. I encourage you to invest the time to get past the façade, and, with your website mission and strategy in hand, to truly understand what skills, talents, and expertise you will require. Then evaluate vendors based on their ability and interest to help you achieve your end goal. If you have not had a great deal of experience in working with web professionals, it may be worthwhile to enlist the support of an expert to help you create the team capable of building a website that will meet your needs and support your goals. Some will even support you throughout the process. I have provided similar services to numerous clients, assisting them with strategy, definition of requirements, team and vendor selection, contract review, design evaluation, SEO guidance, usability, conversion consulting, as well as pre- and post-live review. You may find expertise that complements that of yourself and your trusted team to assist in a similar capacity.

Lead the Charge

Unfortunately, web professionals are not created equal, and most organizations find this out the hard way. Only after you have defined your website mission and strategy will you be able to articulate what the website must do. By defining requirements, even if from a business perspective only, you enhance your chances of getting what you need from those who will be responsible for website design, programming, UX, SEO, copywriting, and scripting. This could be internal resources, one firm, multiple sources, or all you, if you are really brave and talented.

One of the reasons I wrote this book is that so many businesses have come to me (and others like me) for help after hiring the top web firm in their market, only to find out that they can't compete on the national or industry level.

What you do not know can, and most likely will cost you. This book is designed to dispel some common misconceptions about those who build websites to help you make better decisions about hiring website designers, advertising agencies, programmers, copywriters, and/or SEO consultants. You may even find it helpful to share this book with your team and/or vendors, to create a better understanding of what is driving your decisions and what your expectations will be.

Whether you are responsible for the website for a brand you own or manage or for that of a client, it is imperative that you own the website vision and be able to articulate it clearly to others. I will walk you through the process of identifying exactly what you need, how to ask for it from your team or vendors, and how to get the best possible result from every dollar invested.

Match Specialty with Priority

The *Million Dollar Website* integrates all key functions: great design, SEO, usability, sticky content, calls to action, balance of technology and function, and the ultimate goal of converting visitors to customers. Realistically speaking, however, it may be difficult to find one vendor or solution that delivers all of those features. In fact, I will go so far as to say that I rarely encounter a firm that does all of it well. A highly effective approach to getting the biggest bang for your buck is to create a team. Leveraging the expertise of those with specialties that support your goals is a great way to build the *Million Dollar Website*.

Once you have done the work to define your mission and strategy, you will be able to clearly articulate your needs. This will greatly enhance your ability to choose the best contributors for your project; aligning expertise with objectives will enable you to allocate resources and budget for best results.

Fill in the Gaps

Unless you have a large, well-rounded team of professionals specifically hired for expertise in some aspect of the website, it is likely you will have some gaps between needs and available expertise. These professionals may be able to cultivate skill along the way over time. However, if website performance is mission critical, you can't afford to learn along the way. It is likely you will need the expertise of seasoned professionals to consult, train, and/or guide your team in areas that are not specific strengths.

If your primary goal is to compete in search and you have a great copywriter who just isn't experienced in SEO, you may want to enlist the expertise of a search engine optimization expert to optimize content once created or consider training for your copywriter for maximum benefit over time. Or, perhaps you have a good designer, but that individual has no search engine experience; they too can be guided by an SEO, marketing, and/or usability expert, or obtain training to ensure the website design leverages best practices in search-ability, as well as usability, accessibility, and conversion.

If style and design are vital to your brand but your current website falls short of your vision or isn't quite enough to go head-to-head with competitors, seek out the design resources that best reflect your brand to contribute to website design.

If accessibility and usability for a specific audience is a priority, seek out an expert. Truth be told, your website should integrate all functions in every phase of the website.

Whole Is Better than the Sum of Its Parts

You can have a great design, but if it is built upon a platform not supported by devices your customers use, fails to be indexed by search engines, does not offer value or promote conversion visitors to customers, the website is most definitely not a winner.

You must have it all. The website doesn't have to be perfect to be effective. To become a winner, however, the website must integrate a balance of what we know to contribute to high performance and ROI.

What to Look for When Building Your Website Team

Everyone has their own motivation for working on your website, whether it is billable hours, earning a project fee, building a client list (to help them get more clients like you), add a new website to their portfolio, cultivate or promote talent and skill, or to compete for awards.

As we discussed in the chapter "Is Your Website a Money Pit or a Money Tree," most professionals in the web industry view the website as a project rather than a destination to promote interaction and transactions. It is in their best interest to build the website in the most expeditious, profitable manner possible. Their approach to your digital footprint is that of a "project" that has a beginning and an end.

Don't get me wrong—there is nothing wrong with this approach, for them. They are in the business to make money. Their primary objective is volume and keeping cost down. For example, many organizations will sell services sold on the talent of their most talented resources, but then assign it to lesser qualified or talented individuals at a fraction of the cost. This is quite common in advertising agencies, new media firms, design firms, and other organizations. And, although this works quite well in generating profit for them, it doesn't always result in your website getting the attention you believe you are paying for when you select that vendor.

Be Proactive

Knowing about such practices enables you to make specific requests about how your investment will be managed by a vendor. If you find yourself leaning toward an establishment because of a particular level of functionality or perhaps because of the design of a particular piece in their portfolio, don't be afraid to define these specific requirements in your agreement with a vendor.

For internal resources, success is often measured by their ability to meet deliverables on time and in budget. This is fine if your primary goal is to simply push a website live. However, those who care about the quality of the experience, the long-term impact on the investment for the business, often find themselves outnumbered when fighting for cost-efficient, quality solutions. A friend of mine who is a software architect in the financial services industry has expressed repeated frustration with such conflict within his organization. As a senior executive with a personal commitment to excellence, he cares more about performance than those who will simply be accountable for completion of the deliverable. In such scenarios, it may make sense to construct incentive for performance instead of mere completion of the website.

Given the time, energy, and resources required to build a website, the business owner, shareholders, and stakeholders will expect a far greater return on the investment than those without skin in the game. It is pretty safe to say that just by virtue of reading this book; you seek results from the online extension of your business.

One Leader

Every team has a captain; every army has a general. As with any team effort, someone needs to lead. Whether your team will be in-house, outsourced, or some combination thereof, the work you have done and will do to define the website mission and strategy will be extremely valuable in articulating your goals and getting everyone on the same page.

When I work with client agencies, web design firms, marketing firms, developers, and other resources, it is imperative that the client be able to convey their goals consistently to all contributors.

If you ARE the team, or if you plan to hire a professional or consultant along the way to help you build your website, the same process applies.

Following recommendations outlined in this book will enable you to articulate your objectives clearly and promote collaboration that will support your goals. Own the process and the outcome. Investing the time and energy on the front end will enable you to lead with confidence.

Chapter 28:

Administration

The more established your brand becomes the greater visibility it will gain in the digital marketplace. You must include a strategy to reach customers unfamiliar with your brand if you expect to continually grow. (We covered this in depth in the chapters on Website Design, Content, and SEO.)

Not understanding how well the website is working, or not working, and how to fix it, is a vulnerable position far too many businesses and brands place themselves in after building a website.

Ralf Schwoebel, a Multi-national Internet Entrepreneur and Owner of Tradebit.com shares his insight on how accessible and valuable website monitoring tools are:

"There are many, many tools out there. The internet has grown-up and we can use tools to monitor if the site is up, if the site is hacked, website performance, and tools that...check who is linking to you, and who is linking to your competitors so can evaluate what you need to do – to get more traffic."

Stayin' Alive

Monitoring a website is vital in today's ever-changing landscape—not just because the environment in which your website will operate changes, but also because innocent mistakes can have dire consequences.

Down for the Count

Take, for example, one of my clients whose website developer had inadvertently omitted the robots.txt file during a hardware upgrade. They had no knowledge of the problem, and it would have gone unchecked if I had not accessed website data and noticed that the site's traffic had plummeted. After eliminating "blacklisting" by Google as a cause (phew!) the source of the problem was identified.

What happened? Because the robots.txt file was removed, Google could no longer "see" the website and had removed any record of the website in any of its search engine results. It had essentially erased any trace of the website, which was very bad timing as the company was launching an extensive television campaign and operating in a highly competitive consumer category. This was "fixable," but the damage was done, and correcting mistakes like this do not always, or immediately, return the website to its former position in search engine results.

All Data Is Not Created Equal

Reports maintenance programs from vendors are far too often a regeneration of Google Analytics reports with no analysis, interpretation, or recommended actions based on the data. It is easy to push out data. What you do with what the data reveals will determine whether the performance of your website can be improved over time.

Website Analytics

Hopefully you have Google Analytics or Omniture, Web Trends, AND Webmaster Tools—some sort of analytics program—running on your website. If you do not, I highly recommend you implement both an analytics solution and Google Webmaster Tools. Each offers a different view into the data. You can learn how to interpret and apply the insight you need later if you are not yet familiar with it, but whatever you do, be sure to create the accounts and apply the code necessary to generate the data as directed to the website immediately as it goes live.

Which program(s) you select will depend on your goals and how large and/or sophisticated your website will have to be to serve those goals. If you aren't running either program, I would recommend Google Analytics first as it is free and provides the data required to make informed decisions about your website investment.

This is VERY important. The organization must own its data. Your website vendor does not own your business, so it should not own your website (a business asset) or the data that the website generates. It is imperative that you create and/or require your organization be primary owner of website analytic tools being used to monitor your website. I cannot tell you how often clients find out after the fact that the account was created by their agency, web designer, developer, etc. using their email account. With Google Analytics and Webmaster Tools this is major problem because Google, who provides these services, uses the email account to identify the owner. Google does not enable transfer of ownership and does not get involved in ownership management or disputes.

Create Your Own Accounts

If your vendor adds your website to the list of websites that they own, instead of adding analytics that you own to their Client Center, which Google provides to properly administer analytics for multiple websites that one does not own, they will not be able to add you as an administrator because then you would be able to access the analytics of other clients' websites as well as your own. More importantly, you do not own your website data—they do.

The bottom line is, unless you create the account, you do not own the data. This may sound like common sense, but far too many times I have had clients feel great about having their vendor implement Google Analytics for their website only to find out later that they either have no access to the data, they lose access to the data if they change vendors, or they are a permissioned user rather than an administrator, subject to the permission and oversight of the data by others.

The Importance of a Non-Personal Company Email Address

Website data belongs to the organization. Do not let any one employee or vendor create a Google account on your behalf with their email address. Google does not facilitate ownership transfers. So, if that person leaves your organization, you sell it, or you have allowed someone outside the organization to create the account, you will lose historical data. This is no small issue. To maintain ownership of your data, and facilitate use of other Google tools on behalf of the company, use a company account that does not belong to one person (like info@, website@, administrator@, etc.) to which you can control access and will always own.

When you own the website, you take ownership of all assets related to the website. This includes the tools that monitor or generate reports created by access to your website (like Google Webmaster Tools).

Best practices for Google Analytics and Webmaster Tools

Your organization should be the owner and primary administrator of the Analytics accounts, without exception.

Use an email account that is not specific to one person, even if you are the sole owner or user. People come and go, businesses are bought and sold. So, either create an account specifically for this purpose, or use an account that multiple people within your organization can access.

DO NOT provide your administrator username and password to anyone else within or outside of your organization. Instead, give them permission by adding them as either an administrator or user, depending on their role and your level of confidence and trust in them.

Think about it for a moment: If a general mechanic works on one car and only serviced it once every two or three years, how knowledgeable would you expect them to be in servicing the electronics in your brand-new vehicle? The web works the same way. Those tasked with a new website or website redesign are practitioners with other responsibilities and expertise. For most organizations, the website comes into focus once every two, three, or more years. Unless you are living and breathing website design, development, optimization, and measurement, you may lack the perspective needed to create a unique powerful, memorable user experience capable of supporting their goals—I have written this book to provide you with a better perspective.

Chapter 29:

Winning Hearts and Minds

As we near the end of the book, I want to pull it all together for you in a way that will help you act on what you've learned and view the conversion of each visitor to customer with a new perspective.

The primary goal of your website is to help your brand win the hearts and minds of customers, one visitor at a time. That is all you have. Each visitor will determine, based on their experience, how well your brand (service, product, information) meets their needs. When one customer is delighted, they tell others. When they are less than delighted, they tell others, and so on.

Covet the Relationships You Earn

This is a very important topic, so I want you to pay particular attention. You may not realize how little access you have to the relationships you have worked so hard to establish on various social media platforms. Access and the ability to "download" or extract your connections, contacts, friends, etc. from social media platforms, especially Facebook, has become increasingly difficult.

I wrote explicitly about this topic in a blog post entitled *"Who Owns Your Social Network?"*, which I highly recommend for anyone who values the networks created on social platforms.

Extract and Back-Up Data and Assets from Third-Party Platforms

Many do not realize this until it is too late, but in early 2012 Facebook eliminated the ability for Facebook users to download or export their social contacts from Facebook.com. Because the Terms of Service for social media platforms have historically changed so often, your objectives will be best served if you use the platform to make the connection and then gather the data necessary to cultivate those relationships from your own website. And, where there is data to be found (connections on LinkedIn, Circles or contacts on Google+, followers on Twitter, etc.), be sure to export or download it frequently. You never know when that data may become unavailable to you. Remember, it is their *Million Dollar Website* you are participating in, so you are subject to the rules they create.

- Brand digital assets whenever possible (linking to your website where allowed).

- Integrate your own digital assets into your presence on other platforms as naturally and often as you can.

- When sending email, don't provide the entire story or post it on the email program website. Create it, then point to a page on your website designated to receive the clicks, always, even if it is existing content.

By entertaining most interaction on your website, you not only have the opportunity to create a stronger relationship with the visitor, you also gain invaluable data with every click and action they make. This data is invaluable in measuring performance, making design decisions, launching marketing campaigns, determining ROI on PPC campaigns, and as a reference for invaluable data to make informed decisions that will guide the next version of your *Million Dollar Website*.

Should you build a Facebook Store? This will depend on how large your following is on Facebook and whether you feel that you would lose the sale if you were to launch a campaign on Facebook or other mediums and then ask fans to visit your website. You will have to weigh the benefit with the trade-off and make the decision that is right for your brand, goals, and the current situation.

She Told Two Friends, and so On

Did you ever see the Fabergé Organics Shampoo commercial from the 1970s? This commercial conveyed this concept perfectly. One lovely lady states that she liked the shampoo so much that she told two friends, and they told two friends, who told two friends, and so on. The video conveys this concept visually quite well. I've shared a link to the "she told two friends" video on MillionDollarWebsite.TV so you may see for yourself.

See Conversion as the Beginning

With each heart and mind you win, you create a relationship, which opens the door of opportunity to win the hearts and minds of everyone else that individual influences.

Many websites fail to recognize this opportunity and instead see the "purchase" as the final outcome. Nothing could be farther from the truth. The sale is the beginning of a relationship that can and should be coveted. After all, you've invested quite a bit to win that customer, have you not? You must have heard the saying, "It's easier to keep a customer than to get a new one." This is true, but not merely on the merit of preserving that single customer. The art of preventing a customer from defecting to a competing brand will preserve that relationship, and is also likely to generate referrals and recommendations to those they influence. This is especially true in today's social economy.

The Power of One

When you understand how powerful each and every individual customer can be, everything you invest to apply and implement to acquire one customer suddenly becomes more valuable. The cost of customer acquisition is not measured by one, but rather one plus everyone that person influences.

Tap into Spheres of Influence

I am writing a book on this topic. *Spheres of Influence* explains how brands can embrace the inherent power of relationships created by the microcosms in which each of us lives, works, and plays.

For the purpose of creating a high-performance website, let me share with you how spheres can decrease the cost of customer acquisition and greatly expand each conversion by building on the relationship with each customer.

We humans are social creatures. We were long before social media and we always will be, even as many relationships become virtual in nature. As we move through life, we create affinity relationships with others by association, and each sphere has a slightly different dynamic, yet we play a role in each sphere, enabling us to influence others.

Spheres are created by sharing a common interest or goal. The spheres in which we operate are dynamic, reflecting the path of our lives. Your family is a sphere and may have multiple spheres within it: immediate family, extended family, French-speaking family members, in-laws, those in town, out of town, those you look forward to seeing, and those "not so much."

You also develop influence in spheres based on professional interests such as peers with similar roles, co-workers, employees, those in your industry, or those who specialize in specific topics such as orthopedic surgery, public relations, trademark law, urban architecture, mobile app development, SEO, PHP—you get the idea. In addition to professional affiliations, you create spheres of influence through life stages and experiences, such as being a mom, new parent, parent of a teenager, parent of kids who play soccer, grandparent, aunt, military service member, care-giver of a disabled veteran, empty nester, or retiree.

There are unstructured spheres created spontaneously on cruise ships, trains, commercial jets, at restaurants, events, concerts, and other places, such as Times Square at midnight, the Super Bowl, and gatherings such as conferences, shopping malls, and even specific stores such as Best Buy on Black Friday. These spheres are spontaneous because you did not have personal knowledge of a sphere created by strangers sharing a space at a specific time.

Of course there are more formal affiliations, such as groups you participate in—book clubs, poker games, cooking classes, golf partners, places of worship, travel groups, singles groups, volunteers, volunteer firefighters, quilters, etc. Across each of these relationships there may be additional spheres, which create relationships on another level. For example, if you are based in Silicon Valley, you share an affinity with professionals in that geographic market, which creates a natural introduction to others in the sphere and the countless spheres that those individuals belong to.

The spheres of influence for each individual are different, yet they cross over to spheres of influence of countless others, creating a natural affinity with those related to each of those individuals. When you think about your ideal customers, they become a sphere, yet each brings with them a unique collection of relationships based on the spheres created by the story of their lives. When you win the loyalty and trust of that ideal customer, you may find that others in their spheres will be influenced by their decision to choose your brand.

We interact, communicate, and act slightly different with each sphere in which we have influence. Think about it—how you communicate and interact with your friends from college is most likely very different from how you communicate with your immediate family or professional peers. The same is true when you are communicating online.

We have multiple interests that create relationships based on affinities that create spheres in which your brand can gain exposure—influence.

What would you want to see or hear that would differentiate the experience, instill trust, or compel you to take action? This is where your website can transform the concept from you telling your story, to enabling others to tell it for you.

As you identify which mechanisms will best support your website, remember to integrate at the completion of a conversion the invitation for each new customer to post feedback and/or tell their friends about their experience with your website and brand. You could also follow up with an email one week, month, or year after the sale to invite them to post feedback. This all depends on the life cycle of your product or service and can easily be automated through a CRM system or simply managed through email auto-responders triggered by each individual conversion. You can deliver a personal thank you, gift, personalized communication, exclusive access to assets such as whitepapers, video, training, and/or a timed sequence of special offers related to posting reviews, sharing their purchase experience on social media, or a special offer they can send to colleagues, friends, and family (their spheres) that enables them to invite those they influence to become your customers too. We're talking about people who may never have been introduced to your brand without the personal invitation of that customer you have just earned.

You can accept the sale and move on to the next. Or, you can use each website conversion as a building block to build a relationship with that customer and those they influence. What you do once you make the sale determines whether you have just scored a sale—or customer for life.

The choice is yours.

Bibliography

Allen, C. (n.d.). *How Journalists Use Media to Find Stories and Information.* Retrieved from California Green Solutions: http://www.californiagreensolutions.com/cgi-bin/gt/tpl.h,content=1360

Cision. (2010, January 10). *National Survey Finds Majority of Journalists Now Depend on Social Media for Story Research.* Retrieved from Cision.com: http://us.cision.com/news_room/press_releases/2010/2010-1-20_gwu_survey.asp

Fleishman Hillard. (2012, January 31). *Agency News: 2012 Digital Influence Index Shows Internet as Leading Influence in Consumer Purchasing Choices.* Retrieved from Fleishman Hillard: Who We Are: http://fleishmanhillard.com/2012/01/31/2012-digital-influence-index-shows-internet-as-leading-influence-in-consumer-purchasing-choices/

Hoff, T. (2009, July 25). *Latency Is Everywhere and It Costs You Sales - How to Crush It.* Retrieved from High Scalability: http://highscalability.com/latency-everywhere-and-it-costs-you-sales-how-crush-it

Jarboe, G. (2010, April 12). *Google Using Site Speed in Web Search Ranking.* Retrieved from Search Engine Watch: http://searchenginewatch.com/article/2050994/Google-Using-Site-Speed-in-Web-Search-Ranking

Keynote Systems, Inc. (2012). *2012 Mobile User Survey.* Keynote Systems, Inc.

KISSmetrics. (2012). *How Loading Time Affects Your Bottom Line.* Retrieved from KISSmetrics: http://blog.kissmetrics.com/loading-time/?wide=1

Pew Research Center. (2012, February). *Trend Data (Adults).* Retrieved from Pew Internet & American Life Project: http://www.pewinternet.org/Static-Pages/Trend-Data-%28Adults%29/Online-Activities-Daily.aspx

Singhal, A. (2012, May 16). *Introducing the Knowledge Graph: things, not strings.* Retrieved from Google: Official Blog: http://googleblog.blogspot.com/2012/05/introducing-knowledge-graph-things-not.html

Towers, D. (2012, August 23). *PPC accounts for just 6% of total search clicks [infographic].* Retrieved from Econsultancy Digital Marketing Excellence: http://econsultancy.com/us/blog/10586-ppc-accounts-for-just-6-of-total-search-clicks-infographic

Thank you!

For additional resources, visit
MillionDollarWebsites.TV

Join website discussions on
Million Dollar Websites
Google+ and **LinkedIn Groups**